WHY WE BELIEVE THE BIBLE

by
GEORGE W. DEHOFF

McLoud, OK:
Cobb Publishing

2016

ISBN-13: 978-0692673188
ISBN-10: 0692673180

CHANGES MADE IN THIS EDITION

1. Spelling (outside of quotations of Scripture) has been updated to modern usage. For example, words like "realise" are now spelled "realize." This is also true for much of the Old English spelling, which has also been updated to modern spelling. For example, instead of "minde," we now read "mind."

2. Because of the change in page size and text type, the page numbering will not match with the original printed version.

3. Quotations have been set off by indenting the entire quotation.

4. Lists which appear in paragraphs have been set apart in a numbered list like the one which appears on this page.

5. **Bold** font has been added to headings and lists to make them stand apart.

TABLE OF CONTENTS

WHY WE WANT TO BELIEVE THE BIBLE

Recently, I asked a college friend if he believed the Bible. "Why should a fellow want to believe the Bible?" he answered. "What difference does it make anyway?" This, I am persuaded, is the attitude of many, so I give attention to his question.

1. I want to believe the Bible because it teaches that I will live after death.

With other books death is the end of man. With the Bible it is a beginning. Millions of books are in the great libraries of the world. None save the Bible teach that man as the same conscious personality the same individual lives after death. Others have said that man's goodness lives on, or that his spirit is reincarnated and becomes a rock, an insect, a cow or a donkey but the Bible alone advances the idea that the same individual lives again (Jno. 5:28-29).

Every sane individual wants to live beyond death. No man wants to go down into the darkness of the tomb to come up no more. Therefore, every normal individual should want to believe the Bible.

2. I want to believe the Bible because I want to go to a better home than this.

Many books have told of utopias. Only one book has ever seriously told man that he might dwell at last in an ideal abode. That book is the Bible.

We live in a wonderful world. Its joys and friendships grow sweeter as the years go drifting by. Yet, who has not seen poverty, crime, sin, suffering and distress on every hand? Who has not wished that he might dwell where all such is banished?

The Bible teaches that in that fairest of summerlands there will be no death, no pain and no sorrow for "the former things are passed away."

Yes, I want to believe the Bible!

3. I want to believe the Bible because I want to meet my friends who've gone before.

I have known and loved some of earth's finest friends. Some have passed on. I would like to see them again. To me, seeing them again is no more unreasonable than meeting them the first time. I want to see again the friendly smile and clasp again the friendly hand. The Bible is the one book that teaches I may do this.

Ah yes, I want to believe the Bible. It does make a difference!

4. I want to believe the Bible because I have always been taught that it is the truth.

One should not believe something just because he has always been taught that it is the truth. Yet, when one has been taught something so long and so earnestly that it has become a part of his very being, he should not give it up without good and sufficient reason. I have always believed that the Bible is God's word. I have found neither good nor sufficient reason for giving up that faith.

5. I want to believe the Bible because the greatest scientists, outstanding philosophers and best men of all ages past have accepted it as God's word.

By the preponderance of evidence we determine the validity of questioned legal documents, settle disputed dates, and ascertain the facts of science. Should we use this method in dealing with the Bible, we would be driven to the irresistible conclusion that it is God's word.

A few notable examples will show us what others have thought of the Bible:

Dr. William Lyon Phelps, noted educator,

> "...I thoroughly believe in a university education for both men and women; but I believe a knowledge of the Bible without a college education is more valuable than a college course without the Bible."

Sir Walter Scott, on his deathbed, "Bring me the Book!" When asked what book he replied, "There is but one Book!"

Dr. Schurman, President of Cornell University,

> "The Bible is the most valuable document in English literature. No man can be called an uneducated man who knows his Bible and no man can be

called an educated man who does not know his Bible."

Andrew Jackson,

"That Book is the rock on which this republic rests."

Thomas Jefferson,

"I have always said, and will always say, that the studious perusal of the sacred volume will make better homes, better citizens, better fathers, and better husbands."

Abraham Lincoln,

"I am profitably engaged in reading the Bible. Take all of this book upon reason that you can and the balance by faith, and you will live and die a better man.

John Quincy Adams,

'The first and almost the only book deserving of universal distinction is the Bible. I speak as a man of the world to the men of the world and I say to you, 'Search the Scriptures'."

Daniel Webster,

"If we abide by the principles taught in the Bible our country will go on prospering, but if we and our posterity neglect its instruction and authority, no man can tell how sudden a catastrophe may overwhelm us and bury us and our glory in profound obscurity."

Theodore Roosevelt,

"Almost every man who has by his life work added to the sum of human achievements of which the race is proud, almost every such man has based his life work largely upon the teachings of the Bible."

Woodrow Wilson,

"A man has deprived himself of the best there is in the world who has deprived himself of a knowledge of the Bible."

Napoleon Bonaparte, Emperor of France,

"Behold it upon the table. I never fail to read it, and every day with the same pleasure....Not only is one's mind absorbed, it is controlled and the same can never go astray with this book for its guide."

Lord Roberts,

"You will find in this book guidance when you are in health, comfort when you are in sickness and strength when you are in adversity."

Isaac Walton, English author,

"Every hour I read you it kills a sin or lets a virtue in to fight it."

Jean Jacques Rousseau, French philosopher and author,

> "I must confess to you that the majesty of the scriptures astonishes me;...if it had been the invention of man, the invention would have been greater than the greatest heroes."

Charles A. Dana, American journalist,

> "Of all books the most indispensable and the most useful, the one whose knowledge is the most effective is the Bible. There is no book like the Bible. In every controversy the Bible contains the right answer and pleads for the right policy."

John Ruskin,

> "Read your Bible. Make it your daily business to obey it in all you understand. To my early knowledge of the Bible I owe the best part of my tests for literature."

Immanuel Kant, German metaphysician,

> "The existence of the Bible as a book for the people is the greatest benefit which the human race has ever experienced."

David J. Brewer, U.S. Supreme Court,

> "This American nation from its first settlement at Jamestown to this hour is based on and permeated by the principles of the Bible."

Thomas Henry Huxley, English biologist,

> "The Bible has been the Magna Charta of the poor and oppressed; down to modern times no state has a constitution in which the interests of the people are so largely taken into account; in which the duties so much more than the privileges of the rulers are insisted on....Nowhere is the fundamental truth that the welfare of the state in the lone rim depends on the welfare of the citizens so strongly laid down."

Isaac Newton,

> "I account the scriptures of God the most sublime philosophy."

Patrick Henry,

> "There is a Book worth all other books in the world!"

I want to agree with the great and good men who have said, "The Bible is God's word." The human mind is so constituted that it believes only when sufficient evidence is brought to bear upon it. We must, therefore, have some reason for believing the Bible, some evidence upon which to base our faith. As we search for that evidence much will depend on whether we do it with a pro-religious bias, an irreligious bias, or with an open mind. To be open-minded does not mean to open the doors and windows of your mind so that all of the trash in the country may blow in. It does mean to examine carefully the evidence found.

There is abundant reason why one should want to believe the Bible. Let us search, therefore, for evidence which will lead us to believe it.

WHY WE BELIEVE IN GOD

Can we prove the existence of God? Not to a man who does not want to see nor to one who is incapable of seeing, but can we demonstrate to the fully developed, studious man standing in the light of this age arguments which will lead him to believe in the existence of God?

1. We believe in God because Atheism, the only other alternative, cannot be proved.

Every atheist occupies a forced position. Over him will always hang the possibility that there is a God. He alone claims to believe he has no maker, no creator. Before one can proclaim "There is no God" he ought to have made extensive explorations in heaven and earth, in the material world and the spiritual world, in time and eternity. Before a man can know there is no God he would himself have to become one—he would have to be omniscient or the one thing he did not know might be that God exists.

2. We believe in God because it is reasonable to believe that the eternal existence is God—not matter.

A skeptic recently told me not to be guided by the Bible when seeking to learn of the eternal existence but to be guided by reason. It did not occur to him that the Bible might be reasonable or that perfect reason cannot be manifested by man who has always demonstrated his imperfection. Nevertheless, let us take his advice and see what reason teaches us.

Something is, therefore something always was. Had there ever been a time when nothing existed then nothing could have existed at any time for something cannot come from nothing. Had nothing existed, there could have been no event for there would have been no cause. These statements are axiomatic. Something has existed from all eternity.

There are but two things in existence—mind and matter. (Force is not an entity but the energy manifested by one or the other). As to the eternal existence but three things can be supposed: Dualism, which says both mind and matter are eternal; Materialism, which says that matter is eternal and mind is a result of certain combinations and properties of matter; and Theism, which affirms that mind is eternal and that matter is a creation of mind.

Dualism is unscientific. To suppose two eternal existences would solve no difficulty and would give us all the difficulties of Atheism and Theism. The great majority of thinkers have discarded Dualism and divided themselves into two groups. One group supposes that matter is eternal and has created mind, intellect and life; the other group supposes that mind—Almighty God—has existed from all eternity and has created the material universe. Which position is the more reasonable?

It is reasonable to believe that this eternal force was mind, not matter.

> (1) Mind is superior to matter. Mind knows but matter is the object known. Mind moves and modifies matter. Matter is the servant of mind. The

chemist is greater than the chemicals which he handles and the mind is greater than the body which it guides and perhaps destroys.

(2) That which existed from all eternity has spontaneity and force. Without spontaneity it would have remained dormant, without force it would have caused no event. Mind possesses these qualities. It can move bodies and cause events. Matter is destitute of these qualities. Matter remains in the condition in which it is, whether of rest or motion, until something from without changes it. Matter could have produced no change in its eternal state of rest or motion. If we are free to entertain a theory as to the eternal existence why entertain the one least likely to be the truth

(3) The one original existence must have had of her attributes which mind possesses but which matter does not possess. There must have been in this original being all that is developed and manifested in the universe. It possessed the power to think, plan and feel. It had the capacity to love and to hate, to make moral distinctions, to choose between right and wrong. It cannot be proved that matter possesses these attributes in any degree. These powers do inhere in mind. Mind, therefore, was eternal and not matter. (The principal objection to this line of reasoning has been the childish suggestion that we do not know the difference between mind and matter. Certainly we do not know all about either but we do know something about both. They have some attributes in common as do

all things which exist. The fact of existence is one point in common. Matter is known by its qualities, mind by its activities; consciousness reveals the one, the senses the other; one is dead, the other alive; one is senseless, the other full of thought and feeling; one is passive, the other active; one is amenable to physical law, the other to intellectual and moral law. It is as reasonable to question the existence of matter as to question the existence of mind. Indeed, some philosophers have insisted that matter exists only as phenomena revealed in the mind).

3. We believe in God because be universe exhibits marks of intelligent causation.

All the works of man are examples of causation. We see a house and we know it has a builder. "Every house is builded by some man," and though we never find the builder, yet we will know he exists. I look at my watch. It had an intelligent maker. He possessed power. These things are self-evident. Though I never see that watch-maker, yet I know he existed and I know something about him from the product he made. In the same way, we may know that God exists and we may know some-thing about Him by seeing the things which He has made.

Did the electric system of your city and of the nation have a maker? Then what of man's brain and spinal cord with nerves running to every part of the body? Did the telescope "just happen," did it "just make itself"? If not, how could the human eye make itself? Is there an intelli-gent cause for the water system running to all parts of the city? Then what of the system of veins and arteries throughout the body?

Look into the sky. In the day there is the proud monarch of the sky who shakes off the sleep of night and makes his journey through space. He operates with mathematical precision. At night with the naked eye one may see as many as six thousand stars. With the telescope one may see millions of stars and suns flaming like archangels on the frontiers of stellar space. They do not run into one another. They do not go by chance. Men may judge planetary movement of the future by that of the past. Our closest neighbor among the starry host is twenty-five trillion miles away. The light which left this star (Alpha) five years ago is just now reaching the earth having been travelling all this time at the rate of 186,000 miles per second. Pollux, the brighter star of the twins, is thirty-two light years from the earth, a distance of 192,000,000,000,000 miles! Astronomers by present methods of calculation are able to measure a distance of 15,000 light years or 100,000,000,000,000,000 miles out into space. An astronomy teacher once said, "This shows that there is not a great God watching over one little planet called the earth." To which I replied, "On the contrary, it shows how great God is to create and direct so many more things than men formerly supposed." David said, "When I consider thy heavens, the works of thy fingers, the moon and the stars which thou hast ordained; what is man that thou art mindful of him? And the son of man that thou visitest him?" (Psalm 8).

It is said that Benjamin Franklin, while in Paris, made a model planetary system showing the earth and the planets nearest it. Many astronomers copied it to use in their studies. One day an atheist friend saw it and asked, "Who made it?" "No one made it," answered Franklin. "It made itself, it just happened." "What," cried the man, "you're joking." "And so is the man who says the universe just happened," replied Franklin.

Two friends slept in their tent on the desert. One put his head out the following morning and said, "Some camels passed here last night." "How do you know, did you see them?" his friend asked. "Oh no, but I see their tracks," he replied. If we do not see God we see His handiwork and we know He has been here.

An atheist once said, "Show me your God. Let me see, hear, feel, smell or taste him and I will believe." To which a Christian replied, "Show me your brains—let me see, hear, feel, smell or taste them and I will believe." We cannot see life. A man waves his hand and we see the effect of life. We do not hear life. As we speak we hear only the effect of life. We do not feel life. We may feel the pulse of man but that is only the effect of life. Life cannot be demonstrated to the senses. Yet we know men live by the way they behave—and perhaps misbehave. There is life back of the action and though it cannot be demonstrated to the senses yet we believe it exists. In the same way, we know God exists because of the way the universe behaves. There is power back of the orderly arrangement, the evident design and precise operation of the universe.

If the universe exhibits design, there must be a great Designer; if it shows thought, there must be a great Thinker;

if it is run by the laws of nature, there must be a great Lawgiver; if it operates with mathematical precision, there must be a great Mathematician; if the universe gives us important chemical combinations, there must be a great Chemist. Thomas A. Edison said that the universe is such an engineering feat, "There must be a Great Engineer" From these conclusions time is no escape. God exists.

> "I do not have to open the Bible to learn that. (The existence of God). It is enough that I open my eyes and turn them on that great book of nature, where it is legibly written, clearly revealed on every page. 'God'—that word may be read in the stars and on the face of the sun, it is painted on every flower, traced on every leaf, engraven on every rock; it is whispered by the winds, sounded forth by the billows of oceans, and may he heard by the dullest ear in the long-rolling thunder. I believe in the existence of a God, but not in the existence of an atheist, or that any man is so who can be considered in his sound and sober senses. What should we think of one who attempts to account for any other works of beauty and evident design, as he professes to do for those of God? Here is a classic: temple; here stands a statue, designed with such taste and executed with such skill that one almost expects the marble to leap from its pedestal; here bangs a painting of some dead beloved one, so lifelike as to most our tears; here, in 'Iliad' or 'Aeneid' or Paradise Lost', is a noble poem of the grandest thoughts, and clothed in sublimest imagery here is a piece of most delicate, intricate, and ingenious

mechanism. Well, let a man tell me gravely that these were the work of chance; tell me, when I ask who made them, that nobody made them; tell me that the arrangement of letters in this poem, and of the colors in that picture, of the features in the statue, was a matter of mere chance; how should I stare at him? and conclude, without a moment's hesitation, that I had fallen into the company of some drivelling idiot. Turning away from such atheistic ravings about the infinitely more glorious works of God, with what delight does reason echo the closing words of the seraphim's hymn, The whole earth is full of His glory'!" (Guthrie).

4. We believe in God because the moral government of the world implies a moral governor.

Man is a subject of moral government. His conscience tells him there is a right and a wrong and that he ought to do the right. In his heart man believes justice will be done. Since nature knows nothing of justice, there must be One above who will finally mete out justice to all. All guilty men fear the day of retribution. Martyrs to truth and righteousness in every age have committed their cases to a Higher Court. To destroy the belief that right will triumph, that there is a great Moral Ruler who will see that truth does prevail, is to remove the very foundations of moral and social rectitude.

Our faith in God gives promise of victory to those who labor for that which is good; it lets us know that our efforts can never be futile when they are for truth and righteousness; it means that in every storm we can harbor a great tranquility within our souls. Our belief in God means that we will face life optimistically for "this is the victory that overcometh the world, even our faith."

5. We believe in God because the majority of scientific men and philosophers in all ages have believed in God.

Few indeed have been the great thinkers who did not believe in God. Socrates held that the Supreme Being is the immaterial, infinite Governor of all, that the world bears the stamp of His intelligence, that He is the author and vindicator of moral law. Aristotle believed in God, he said, for three reasons: the Ontological, founded on our necessary idea of an eternal existence; the Cosmological, based on the fact that for every effect there must be a cause, back of all harmony there must be intelligence; and the moral argument which has already been given. Copernicus and Galileo believed in God and believed the Bible also. Sir Isaac Newton, who discovered the law of gravity; Joseph Priestley (a preacher) who was co-discoverer of oxygen; Michael Faraday and Lord Kelvin, the great British scientists; Jenner, who discovered the principle of vaccination; our own Robert A. Millikan, who isolated the electron, as well as thousands of other outstanding scientists and philosophers of all time have expressed firm faith in God. Darwin said, "The question of whether there is a creator and leader of the universe has been answered in the affirmative by the greatest spirits that ever lived." lie also said he could not conceive of the origin of life unless God had created it. Thomas A. Edison said, "There is a great directing head of things, a Supreme Being, who looks after the destinies of the world." Sir Charles Lyell, a great geologist, said, "In whatever direction we may turn our investigations, everywhere we are met by the clearest proofs of a creating Intelligence." Such testimonies could be multiplied without limit. We do not seek by sheer authority to prove the existence of God but simply to show that the multitude of common people, all Christian scholars, and all others with only an exception here and there have believed in the existence of God. The man who does not believe in God should be able to show that he has made a more profound study of the evidence than have these men, else, how does he expect to impeach their testimony?

6. We believe in God because of the abundance of the evidence.

Most people believe in God for reasons the sufficiency of which they have never had occasion to question. Yet, the questioning mind can find almost an unlimited number of reasons for believing in God. We decide other questions by the preponderance of evidence. Why not this one? Suggestive of the lines of proof which might be developed, a friend of mine writes that he believes in God for these reasons: Intuitional, Ontological, Cosmological, Geological, Astronomical, Physio-Theological, Psychological, Historical, Providential, and Ethical. Yet skeptics claim they cannot find any line of proof to indicate the existence of God! Shall we say they cannot or will not?

7. We believe in God because all the objections to believing in God lie with equal force against Atheism.

Atheists have objected to a belief in God because, they say, we seek to rise from the finite to the infinite; that from finite reasoning we seek to draw an infinite conclusion. We do, of course, seek to pass from the finite to the infinite in our reasoning. Just as the limited suggests the unlimited; as finite time suggests infinite time and finite space suggests infinite space, so finite intelligence suggests Infinite Intelligence. But the Atheist, since he claims to know that there is no God, believes that matter is eternal, self-existent and infinite. Something is infinite in eternal existence. The Atheist believes it is matter; the Christian believes it is God

Atheists have said that the conception of an intelligent First Cause proves nothing as the First Cause would then need to be accounted for. We do not need to account for the first cause because it is the first cause and there could be no cause back of it. Since we cannot go back of the first cause it is more reasonable to stop at mind than matter. If this be a difficulty, however, Atheism is likewise beset with it, for if matter is the eternal existence what was before it? Matter gives no evidence of self-existence.

Skeptics have objected that we do not know God perfectly. Indeed, we know nothing perfectly. If we knew God perfectly, we would then be gods ourselves. However, matter in none of its forms is known perfectly. If we must know a thing perfectly before we can know it exists, then we cannot know that matter exists. Probably no one will ever understand a being of greater measure than himself. Some men cannot understand how others can be noble, unselfish and sacrificing. They do not have any standards by which to measure them.

Every Objection which an Atheist can make against the existence of God can be made against his belief in the eternal existence of matter.

8. We believe in God because Atheism has insuperable difficulties of its own

The Atheist criticizes the Christian for assuming that God exists. He then assumes the eternal existence of matter, that the forces of this world are self-active, that the laws of the universe are eternal, and that nature continually repeats the same cycle of changes (else it would run its course and have become inactive long ago). Atheism assumes that nature exhibits no thought, no design, no plan. Bold indeed are these assumptions and not one of them can be proved.

Atheism assigns an inadequate cause of the universe. Matter does not possess the qualities of thinking, feeling, and volition which we see in the universe. It is, therefore, an inadequate cause of the universe.

Atheism assumes that life came from dead material without outside stimuli. This would be a greater miracle than the resurrection of the dead.

Atheism maintains the absurd position that all things exist as the result of chance. Theists believe in design. The opposite of design is chance, sheer chance. A watch cannot by chance bring itself into existence, neither can a universe. If the pieces of a watch were placed together in a box and shaken for a million years they would not arrange themselves into a watch. The organs of the human body could not have arranged themselves by chance; the design of nature did not just happen, in fact, nothing runs by chance. We are justified, therefore, in believing in an Eternal Mind and in discarding chance (whatever that may be).

9. Intelligent causation and design is always associated with personality. God must, therefore, be a Personality, a divine Being.

There is nothing in nature, there is no known fact, principle or law which disproves the existence of God. Atheism is without foundation. "No syllogism can be formed that will prove it, no experiment performed that will certify it." All we know of intelligent causation and design is associated with a person. We have no knowledge of abstract intelligence. We are, therefore, justified in concluding that God is a divine Personality, a divine Being and not an abstract idea or fact. There is strong resemblance in the design of nature and the design of man. Man looks at the movable joints of his hand and makes a wrench. He observes the valves of the heart and the pulley of the eye and models his invention after them. He sees the great mountains with broad bases and the low center of gravity, and models his pyramids and tall buildings after them. We conclude that as these things are the result of deliberate planning on man's part, the universe is a result of deliberate planning on God's part.

Man must believe in God or in Atheism. These are the two positions challenging our attention. Thomas Jefferson, the one of our Presidents who was inclined to be skeptical, considered the evidence and wrote his friend,

John Adams, "An Atheist I can never be." It is more logical to believe in God than not to believe. It is difficult to believe sometimes but far more difficult not to believe. Shall we say, "In the beginning matter created all things" or "In the beginning Eternal Nothing created all things" or shall we say, "In the beginning God created the heavens and the earth"?

(For some of the material in this chapter I am indebted to the works of H. W. Everest, principally his book, The Divine Demonstration).

Genesis 1

THE AGE of the earth is a profound secret hidden in 1. the depth of the eternal ages and known only to Almighty God. The Bible does not give the date of creation nor does it suggest anything which will enable us to ascertain this date. Some have erroneously stated, "The first chapter of Genesis says the earth was created about six or seven thousand ,years ago," while the first chapter of Genesis says no such thing. Granting that the events of the six days of Genesis 1 occurred six thousand years ago, we are still face to face with the fact that the heavens and the earth were not created on the first—nor any other—of these days. The heavens and the earth were created before the first day. "In the beginning God created the heavens and the earth" (Gen. 1:1). How long this was before the first day which begins in Genesis 1:3 no one knows. Do some suppose that the earth had existed for millions of years? Certainly it did not exist before the beginning and that is when Moses said it was created. If it took millions of years for beds of coal to form and if our crude oil has been "mellowed 100 million years," Genesis 1 is still correct. It should be borne in mind, however, that God could have created these things instantly and He may have done so. No man knows whether the earth was created a billion years before the first day of Genesis 1 or whether it was created ten seconds before. We do know that "IN THE BEGINNING GOD CREATED the heavens and the earth." "He spake and it was done; He commanded and it stood fast" (Psalms 33:9).

First Condition of the Earth.

Moses tells us (Genesis 1:2) that "the earth was without form and void and darkness was upon the face of the deep." This is evidently not its original condition but its condition just before God "made," reconstituted or renewed the earth and prepared it as a dwelling place for man during the six days of Genesis 1.

> "As to what the condition of the earth was when it was first created, what were its inhabitants, if any, during that remote period, the Bible furnishes but little information, as such matters have necessarily only an indirect bearing upon God's revelation to man." (Sidney Collet, All About the Bible, p. 250).

Robert Milligan says,

> "When this beginning (of Genesis 1) was, or how long it occurred before the Adamic epoch, we have no means of ascertaining with any high degree of certainty. But geology makes it quite probable, if not indeed absolutely certain, that it occurred many ages previous to the historic period; and moreover, that during these intervening ages, many distinct orders of vegetables and animals were created and destroyed at the beginning and close of each geological formation....But these matters have no direct connection with the Scheme of Redemption. And hence it is that Moses passes over them all in silence, and simply notices in the second verse of his narrative, the chaotic state of the earth after the last great cataclysm that occurred shortly before

the first day of the Adamic era." (Scheme of Redemption, pp. 24-25).

Some verses of scriptures indicate that the earth was created fair and beautiful beyond our highest imagination. Isa. 45:18 says, "Thus saith the Lord that created the heavens, God himself that formed the earth, He created it not in vain." The word translated "in vain" is exactly the same as that translated "without form" in Genesis 1:2 and the Revised Version translates it "waste" in both places; hence God created the earth "not in vain," "not waste," "not void."

Job 38:4-7 tells us that when God first laid "the foundations of the earth" conditions were such that "the morning stars sang together and all the sons of God shouted for joy" indicating the perfection and completeness of the work of creation. Some have suggested that the Hebrew word for creation "implies that the creation was a perfect work, in perfect and beautiful order."

The words translated "The earth was without form and void" (Gen. 1:2) might equally well be translated "The earth became waste and void" implying as stated in Isaiah 45:18 that it had not always been that way, just as we read in Genesis 19:26 Lot's wife "became a pillar of salt". The words are the same in the original. Rotherham's Emphasized Bible translates the passage "Now the earth had become waste..." The Authorized Version says, "without form and void"; the American Revised, "waste and void"; the Chaldee Version, "But the earth had become desert and empty"; the Aramaic, "And the earth had become ruined and uninhabited"; and the Vulgate says, "dreary and empty."

FIRST INHABITANTS OF THE EARTH.

The length of the period (or periods) before the first day of Genesis 1 and the inhabitants of the earth (if any) is largely a matter of conjecture. These matters can have no bearing on the scheme of redemption as presented in the Bible, hence its writers do not discuss them.

There are scriptures which have led some to conclude that our earth was once the abode of Satan and his angels in their unfallen condition; that they had bodies of some sort and were fair to behold but that Satan led a rebellion against God and His power and God destroyed the earth until it "was waste and void and darkness was upon the face of the deep," that these angels of Satan were cast down and "reserved in chains until judgment."

The scriptures used to support this theory are given here. The expressions translated "waste" and "void" in Genesis 1:2 occur together in only two other places in the Bible Isa. 34:11 translated "confusion" and "emptiness" and Jer. 4:23—and in both places they are used in connection with the judgment of God on account of sin.

Satan is called "the god of this world" (2 Cor. 4:4), "the prince of this world" (Jno. 12:31), "the prince of the power of the air," (Eph. 2:2), and in tempting Christ he laid claim to the kingdoms of this world (Luke 4:5-8). The prophecy of Ezekiel 28:12-19 may be a glimpse of Satan under the titles of "King of Tyrus" (ver. 12) and "the anointed cherub" (ver. 14) when he in his pristine glory was set upon "the holy mountain of God" "full of wisdom and perfect in beauty" (ver. 12). These words would hardly be applied to any man. Afterward in his "iniquity" (ver. 15) "slander" and "pride" (ver. 17) he was "cast out" (ver. 16). The expression "cast out" was frequently used in connection with evil spirits. "How art thou fallen from heaven O Lucifer, son of the morning!" (Isa. 14:12).

If this be the meaning of that prophecy, then it is clear why the sin of pride, haughtiness and arrogance is especially detestable in the sight of God. "Pride, arrogancy and the evil way—do I hate." (Prov. 8:13). Pride is especially called "the condemnation of the devil" (1 Timothy 3:6). Again, "Pride goeth before destruction and an haughty spirit before a fall" (Prov. 16:18).

The pre-Adamic destruction of the earth and heavenly bodies seems to be vividly described in Job 9:4-7, "He is wise in heart, and mighty in strength; who hath hardened himself against Him and hath prospered? Which removeth the mountains and they know not: which overturneth them in His anger. Which shaketh the earth out of her place, and the pillars thereof tremble. Which commandeth the sun, and it riseth not; and sealeth up the stars."

If the sun "riseth not" and the stars are sealed up, then naturally the earth "became waste and void and darkness was upon the face of the deep." The withdrawal of the light of the sun would, within two days, bring down every atom of moisture from the air in deluges of rain and

piles of snow. A universal frost would cover the earth
and the temperature would reach two or three hundred
degrees below zero. All life and probably even that within the germs of seeds would quickly be destroyed. This
seems to have been the condition of the earth when we
have it first presented to us in Genesis 1. It was "waste
and void," perhaps a great ice age gripped it and "darkness was upon the face of the deep.

THE EARTH PREPARED FOR MAN.

At the end of Genesis 1:2 the reconstitution (erroneously
called the creation) of the earth begins. Man and all living creatures were created (Gen. 1:21) but the earth, created perhaps ages before, was now renewed as we read in
Psalms 104:30, "Thou sendest forth thy spirit, and they
(all living creatures) are created; and Thou renewest the
face of the earth."

There is a vast difference between the words "create" and
"make." "To create" is to make something which did not
previously exist while "to make" implies the forming
from existing materials. A tailor makes a coat but he does
not create the coat. The Hebrew word "bahrah" means
absolute creation while the Hebrew word "ahsah" simply
means to make from something already in existence.
These are the words used in Genesis 1. "In the beginning
God created (bahrah) the heavens and the earth" (Gen.
1:1). "In six days the Lord made (ahsah) heaven and
earth" (Exodus 20:11). In Genesis 2:2 we read "On the
seventh day God ended His work which He had made
(ahsah) and He rested from His work which He had made
(ahsah) and He rested on the seventh day from His work

which He had made (ahsah)." On the fourth day God caused the sun, moon and stars to appear in the heavens and made (ahsah) them our timekeepers. There is nothing in the text to indicate that they were just then created. Doubtless they had existed from the beginning as had the earth but were just now made to be our chronometers.

No statement of this matter can be more conclusive than Genesis 2:3 where we read, "God blessed the seventh day and sanctified it; because that in it He had rested from all His work which God created and made." Here we have both words in the same verse.

All the arguments against and attacks on the scriptures based on the time required for the formation of coal and the fossil remains of animals which may have lived on the earth in pre-Adamic times mean nothing even if we accept as correct the far-fetched guesses of pseudo-scientists who sometimes differ as much as a hundred million years about the age of some particular fossil which has been dug up.

It should also be borne continually in mind that an Almighty God who could create Adam full-grown could instantly create a full-grown bed of coal. The Christ who turned water into wine (John 2) and provided bread for the people in a moment (john 6) also created all things (John 1:1) and He could have done it instantly.

THE "DAYS" OF GENESIS 1.

The seven days mentioned in Genesis 1: Were they natural solar days of twenty-four hours each or were they long periods corresponding to millions of years of our time?

The word "day" is sometimes used to mean a period of time as "In the day that the Lord made the earth and the heavens" (Gen. 2:4) and "The day of temptation in the wilderness" (Ps. 95:8). We speak of the day of prosperity.

The Hebrew word for "day" is "yom" and in the Authorized Version of the English Bible is translated more than 1100 times as "day", 67 times as "time", 30 times as "today", 18 times as "forever", 10 times as "continually", 6 times as "age", 4 times as "life", and 2 times as "perpetually". From this it appears that no one would be able to tell from the word "day" (yom) itself how long Moses intended to say each period was.

That the days mentioned by Moses were ordinary solar days of approximately twenty-four hours each is obvious for many reasons. In the first place, these days were half darkness and half light. What other kind of days have ever been thus? (Let it not be objected that the sun and moon were not made until the fourth day as light was brought into existence on the first day and may exist quite independently of the sun).

When a definite number precedes the word "yom" or "day" in scripture a solar day is always meant—never a long period. There were one hundred and fifty days of the flood (Gen. 8:3), forty days the spies were gone (Number 13:25) three days Jonah was in the belly of the fish (Jonah 1:17), and our Lord was seen after His resurrection forty days (Acts 1:3), and the Lord made heaven and earth in six days (Ex. 20:11).

On the third day of Genesis the grass, trees and shrubs were created. If this day was a "long period, perhaps millions of years" how do these things live in darkness for half that period?

God himself settles this question in Exodus 20:8-11, "Remember the Sabbath day to keep it holy. Six days shalt thou labor and do thy work but the seventh is a sabbath unto Jehovah thy God...for in six days the Lord made heaven and earth, and the sea, and all that in them is, and rested the seventh day; wherefore Jehovah blessed the sabbath day and hallowed it." God gave the Jews the seventh day to keep as a sabbath; the original sabbath on which God rested was typical of this, hence both were twenty-four hour days.

(The objection is brought that "God is still resting in His sabbath" but Jesus said, "My Father worketh hitherto and I work (John 5:17). That God "rested" did not imply that He was tired but that He finished the work of Genesis 1 and hence "rested" from it. "God rested on the seventh day" (Gen. 2:2). "God blessed the seventh day and sanctified it, because that in it He had rested" (Gen. 2:3). "God did rest the seventh day" (Heb. 4:4). God's period of rest on the seventh day had already closed when He blessed that day and gave it to Israel as a sabbath).

The day mentioned in Genesis 1 had "evening and morning". The Jews still count time after this fashion, the day beginning at six in the evening, hence each day consists of "evening and morning".

Finally, whoever thought in the first place that it was necessary for God to have long periods of time to do the work which Moses says He did in six days? It seems clear to me that the days of Genesis 1 were solar days of approximately twenty-four hours each.

CONCLUSION.

From this brief study we are led to conclude that Genesis 1 is scientifically accurate and, therefore, ought to be accepted as God's word.

THE ORIGIN OF RELIGION

There is an all-wise God. He is the eternal, self-existent, vitalizing force of the universe; a Personality Who has created and intelligently directs all things. He did not come from anywhere; He has always existed. He is life inherent—the first cause. After bringing order out of chaos and preparing the earth for man, God created man, "male and female created He them".

After man's creation, God revealed to him true religion. He gave man information concerning the character of God and what He wanted man to do; God gave moral laws to govern man's action toward his fellows and positive laws to cause him to retain his faith in God. These laws were so universally planted in the hearts of all people that it has been impossible for the ravages of time and sin to obliterate them. Revealed to the first people who ever lived on earth, they yet live in the heart of man. Later when man was exceedingly corrupt, God spoke to Moses and other prophets revealing additional truth. God dealt with man not as man should have been but as man was, hence these laws had severe penalties attached to them. When it had been thoroughly demonstrated that man could not think his way out of his own troubles nor keep even those laws which a benevolent Heavenly Father had given, God sent His Son into the world to abrogate the old laws and their penalties and to place man under a system of mercy and grace the New Testament law. This is the origin of true religion.

THE DEVOLUTION OF RELIGION.

How could mankind forget a pure religion after it had been revealed?

"This is what I now try to explain. That degeneration I would account for by the attractions which animism, when once developed, possessed for the naughty natural man, 'the Old Adam'. A moral Creator in need of no gifts, and opposed to lust and mischief, will not help a man with love-spells, or with malevolent 'sending' of disease by witchcraft; will not favor one man above his neighbor, or one tribe above its rivals, as a reward for sacrifice which he does not accept, or as constrained by charms which do not touch his omnipotence. Ghosts, and ghost-gods, on the other hand, in need of food and blood, afraid of spells and binding charms, are corrupt, but, to man, a useful constituency. Man being what he is, man was certain to 'go a whoring' after practically useful ghosts, ghost-gods, and fetishes which he could keep in his wallet or 'medicine bag'. For these he was sure, in the long run, first to neglect his idea of his Creator; next, perhaps, to reckon Him as only one, if the highest, of the venal rabble of spirits or deities, and to sacrifice to Him as to them. And this is exactly what happened! If we are not to call it 'degeneration', what are we to call it? It may be an old theory but facts 'winna ding', and are on the side of an old theory. Meanwhile, on the material plane, culture kept advancing, the crafts and the arts arose;

departments arose, each needing a god....But at this stage of culture, the luck of the state, and the interests of a rich and powerful clergy, were involved in the maintenance of the old, animistic, relatively non-moral system, as in Cuzco, Greece and Rome. That popular and political regard for the luck of state, that priestly self-interest (quite natural), could only be swept away by the moral monotheism of Christianity or Islamism. Nothing else could do it. In the case of Christianity the central and most potent of many combined influences, apart from the life and death of our Lord, was the moral monotheism of the Hebrew religion of Jehovah." (Andrew Lang, The Making of Religion, pp. 237-258)

"Every step taken in religion by man since Adam, if it was not in the right line of monotheism, must have been away from the truth of revealed religion; the only evolution, the evolution of error. Man's imagination, when once it abandons the one guide, becomes the prey of all sorts of perversions, of the monstrous customs of heathendom, which it is useless to trace, as they lead only away from the truth. and are as irrational and as little to be heeded as the ravings of a mind distraught." (Frank Byron Jevons, An Introduction to the History of Religion, pp. 4-5).

This devolution continued for hundreds and perhaps thousands of years. Some people, however, did not descend into ignorance and superstition. They retained a knowledge of the original revelation to man. Noah called upon God when the hearts of others imagined only evil and Abraham worshipped one God when others in the Ur of Chaldees called upon their idols. The more enlightened, civilized and intelligent men were, the closer they remained to the original idea of religion. The more ignorant and immoral they became, the more they corrupted this religion with superstition and fancy. It is not to be supposed that all heathen peoples reached the same depths of depravity nor that all people even in one such nation descended to the same depth. Neither should it be thought that each nation started from the same place in thought nor the same time in history. Some peoples learned only of the original patriarchal religion and their present heathen condition is a corruption of that system. Others learned not only of this system but the additional truth taught by Moses. In their present heathen systems are traces of these early revelations. Others in their heathen systems show that they have borrowed ideas also from the religion of Christ and have corrupted them. Thus at different times and places men have left the truth and started down the path to heathenism. The speed with which they travelled and the depth to which they went depended on their ignorance, immorality and hardness of heart.

THE BIBLE ACCOUNT OF DEVOLUTION.

"God made man upright but they have sought out many inventions" (Eccl. 7:29).

"Because that, when they knew not God, they glorified him not as God, neither were thankful, but became vain in their imaginations, and their foolish heart was darkened; professing themselves to be wise, they became fools, and changed the glory of the incorruptible God into an image made like unto corruptible man and birds, and four-footed beasts and creeping things. Wherefore God also gave them up to uncleanness through the lusts of their own hearts, to dishonor their own bodies between themselves; who changed the truth of God into a lie, and worshipped and served the creature more than the Creator who is blessed forever" (Rom. 1:21-25).

According to Paul, the Divine alone is real, all else is error. A society or a nation is progressive in so far as it hears the Divine Voice—all else is degeneration.

> "Nowadays we are all devotees of the theory of development: it is no longer a theory, it has become the basis and guiding principle of our thought and mind: we must see development everywhere. But it is necessary to be very sure first of all that we have got hold of the right law of development in history; and we are sometimes too hasty. We can easily arrange religions in a series from the lowest to the highest, and we are wont to assume that this series represents the historical development of religion from the most primitive to the most advanced. The fetish, the totem and the sacred animals, and so on up step by step to Jehovah and the Ark of the Covenant. Is that the true line?
>
> "You observe that the assumptions here are very serious. Is the modern savage really primitive? Paul would have said that he represents the last

stage of degeneration, that he is the end and not the beginning, that he has lost almost everything that is really primitive, that he has fallen so completely from the ancient harmony with the order of nature and sympathy with the Divine as to be on the verge of death, and an outrage on the world and on human nature. (p. 16).

"Who is right, Paul or the moderns? For my own part, I confess that my experience and reading show nothing to confirm the modern assumptions in religious history, and a great deal to confirm Paul. (Italics mine. G.W.D). Whatever evidence exists, with the rarest exceptions, the history of religion among men is a history of degeneration; and the development of a few Western nations in invention...should not blind us to the fact that among the vast majority of nations the history of manners and civilization is a story of degeneration....Is it not the fact of human history that man, standing alone, degenerates; and that he progresses only where there is in him so much sympathy with and devotion to the Divine Life as to keep the social body pure and sweet and healthy? (p. 17).

"Beginning the study of Greek Religion as a follower of Robertson Smith and M'Lennan, and accepting the Totemist theory as the key of truth, I was forced by the evidence to the view that degeneration is the outstanding fact of religious history, and that the modern theory often takes the last products of degeneracy as the facts of primitive religion." (p. 29). (William Ramsey, Cities of St. Paul).

EVOLUTIONISTIC THEORIES
OF THE ORIGIN OF RELIGION.

"From the older evolutionist times there are many theories about the origin of sacrifice. There is that of Tylor and Wilkens, who derive it from the present made to the chief, the ghosts, or the spirits; there is also that of Hubert and Mauss, going back to that of Tylor; further there is that of Robertson Smith, deriving sacrifice from the totemic communion. W. Wundt makes it proceed from magical action and A. Loisy from a combination of magic presents to ghosts. (pp. 11:12).

"Now if the most favorable view of all these theories is taken, they afford only possibilities...but none of them any scientific certitude whatever. The reason for this lies in the fact that none of them has seriously asked the question regarding the ethnological age of the tribes and peoples from which they take their proofs.

"But if this important question is raised, the following facts result from it with full certitude; the peoples ethnologically oldest knew neither feeding of ghosts, nor giving of presents to spirits, nor totemic communion, nor totemism in general, not magic rites of a kind from which sacrifices could be derived...(p. 12).

"Now the religion of the oldest culture, of which we have a tolerably good knowledge, emphasizes in a quite special degree the creative power of the Supreme Being, and His complete right of owner-ship over the whole world...the belief of these old-est religions is that the Supreme Being has given these things to man for man's use; not to be wast-ed, but to be treated with respect." (p. 13) (W. Schmidt, High God's in North America).

Primitive man, therefore, recognized that all things come from God, that without God's help he could not secure even food and drink, hence within his heart there was a natural desire to offer sacrifices to God.

Lewis Browne, once a rabbi, in a book, This Believing World, says that man's religion is a product of an evolu-tionary process; that it is man's attempt to lift himself by his bootstraps out of savagery. (p. 22). He lists the origin of religions after this fashion: Animism, Shamanism, Fet-ishism, Tabooism and Sacerdotalism. Unfortunately for all who hold this idea, it does not agree with the facts. Experience and history both teach that man, if left to his own devices and resources will go backward spiritually rather than forward; that the only true incentive to moral and spiritual progress is not a pushing power from within but a pulling power from without. My friend, James D. Bales, has well said, "The only thing in which man is self-sufficient is in sinning".

Socrates gave his philosophy, and its essence is that we should seek Self-knowledge. But self-knowledge only reveals to the candid and thoughtful person the depravity of man and his need of a Saviour. Kant's philosophy called for man to be guided by Reason. But pure reason exists only with perfect personality and man has never demonstrated his imperfection. Reason may lead one man to do one thing and another to take an entirely different course. Man's failures and troubles demonstrate that he does not possess and hence cannot be guided by pure reason. Schopenhauer and Nietzsche, the German philosophers, glorify Will under such terms as the "will to power", "the will to live", etc. This is a philosophy of force which has resulted in the heartless military machine of central Europe.

The philosophies of man have proved themselves futile and inadequate. Indeed, someone has said, philosophy is a blind man in a dark cellar trying to catch a black cat which isn't there. La Rochefoucauld said, "Philosophers can easily triumph over the evils that have already passed and the future evils but present evils triumph over the philosophers."

Christ gave His philosophy to the world. This philosophy of Christ calls for Love of God which, if practiced, would banish worldliness, idolatry, blasphemy, profanity, covetousness and such like; it calls for Love of One Another which, if practiced, would eradicate jealousy, divisions, factions, murder, fornication, adultery, theft, enmities, war and such like. This philosophy of Christ is also spiritual. It teaches that the death of Christ is our atonement and makes possible our reconciliation. It presents simple commandments and items of devotion which are applicable to and understood by all classes of mankind.

The Voice of History.

History teaches us that the earliest forms of heathen religions were purer than the later forms. No nation or tribe has been found which did not believe in a Supreme Being of some kind and practice religion in some form. In every heathen system, especially the oldest ones, may be found traces of a once pure monotheism.

Professor Fairburn of Oxford said,

> "The younger the polytheism, the fewer its gods." (Studies in the Philosophy of Religion, p. 22).

Dr. James Orr, Professor of Apologetics and Systematic Theology, United Free Church College, Glasgow, having quoted the above, adds,

> "Man's earliest ideas of God were not, as is commonly assumed, his poorest.—No savage tribes are found who do not seem to have higher ideas of God along with their superstitions. Man does not creep up from fetishism, through polytheism, to monotheism, but polytheism represents rather the refraction of an original undifferentiated sense or consciousness, or perception of the divine.—In theism we find a monotheistic background." (The Problem of the Old Testament, p. 496).

Dr. E. W. Hopkins, Ph.D., LL.D., professor of Sanskrit and Comparative Philology, Yale University, says,

"That all religions may trace back to one primordi-
al religion is not wholly a narrow 'orthodox' view.
In this form, however, it is still held by both the
Hindu and the Christian of every conservative
type. For example, about two thousand years ago,
Manu, the Hindu law-giver, declared, what is still
believed by orthodox Brahmans, that one true religion was revealed to man in the beginning and that
all later types of religion have been vain divergen-
cies from this divine model." (The History of Religions, p. 12).

Dr. William Matthew Petrie, LL.D., Ph.D., etc., Professor
of Egyptology, University College, London, says,

"Were the conception of a god only an evolution
from such spirit worship we should find the worship of many gods preceding the worship of one
god, polytheism would precede monotheism in
each tribe and race. What we actually find is the
contrary of this, monotheism is the first stage
traceable in history. Wherever we can trace polytheism to its earliest stages we find that it results
from combinations of monotheism." (The Religion
of Ancient Egypt, pp. 3-4).

Dr. Hopkins quotes from R. H. Nassau,

"All religions had but one source and that a pure
one. From it have grown perversions varying in
their proportions of truth and error." (Fetishism in
West Africa, p. 23).

Dr. William A. P. Martin of Peking University discusses the evolutionary theory of the origin of religion and adds this significant comment:

> "This theory has the merit of verisimilitude. It in-dicates what might be the process if man were left free to make his own religion; but it has the mis-fortune to be at variance with the facts. A wide survey of the history of civilized nations (and the history of others is beyond reach) shows that the actual process undergone is precisely opposite to that which this theory supposes; in a word, that man was not left to construct his own creed, but that his blundering logic has always been active in its attempts to corrupt and obscure a divine origi-nal." (The Chinese, pp. 163-164).

Professor Max Muller, famous Oxford Professor, said,

> "Whenever we can trace back a religion to its first beginnings we find it free from many of the blem-ishes that offend us in its later phases." (Chips from a German Workshop, Vol. 1, p. 23).

EGYPT.

Dr. Budge, keeper of the Egyptian and Assyrian antiques in the British Museum, says that as late as the Fourth Dynasty only about two hundred gods were worshipped in Egypt. In the Nineteenth Dynasty Thebes alone had about twelve hundred gods and there were hundreds of local gods in other religious centers. Dr. Budge said,

"The sublimer portions are demonstrably ancient; and the last state of the Egyptian religion, that which was known to the Greek or Latin writers, heathen and Christian, was by far the grossest and most corrupt." (Quoted by Renouf in Hibbard Lectures, p. 91).

INDIA.

The Rig-Veda contains the most ancient hymns of India. It shows that the early inhabitants of India believed in one God. A translation of the 129th hymn of the tenth book reads thus:

"In the beginning there was neither naught nor aught
Then there was neither atmosphere nor sky above,
There was neither death nor immortality,
There was neither day nor night, nor light, nor darkness,
Only the **existent One** breathed calmly self-contained,
Naught else but He was there, naught else above, beyond."

BABYLON.

"There are many, nay numberless gods; but they are only revelation forms of the One Great Divine Might." (Dr. Winkler as quoted by On, Problems of the Old Testament, p. 409).

GREECE.

"The Orphic hymns, long before the advent of the popular divinities, celebrated the Pantheos, the

Universal God." (Dr. Martin, quoted by Dr. Ellin-wood, Oriental Religions and Christianity, p. 228).

CHINA. Professor Legge of Oxford says,

"Five thousand years ago the Chinese were mono-theists—not henotheists but monotheists." (The Religions of China, p. 16).

AUSTRALIA. Andrew Lange, speaking of the early ab-origines of Australia, said,

"They believe in a Supreme Being whose abode is in the heavens, and who observes and rewards conduct." (The Making of Religion, p. 189).

NORTH AMERICA.

"The oldest tribes of North America: North-Central Californians, Algonquins, Selish...Now it is pre-cisely among these three oldest primitive peoples of North America that we find a clear and firmly established belief in a High God. a belief which, especially in the oldest of them, the North-Central Californians and the Algonquins, is of quite a par-ticular character by virtue of the high importance attributed to the idea of creation. (p. 19).

"The Supreme Being of the old Maidu religion bears the names Wonomi ('immortal, no death'), Kodo-yapeu ('World-Creator'), Kodo-yanpe ('World-namer'), Kodo-yeponi (World-chief'). He and only he is creator of the whole world. He is the creator of men, whom he forms from the clay: a pair of beings, man and wife, whom he animates. He is more powerful than any other being. It is true that he yields to Coyote his adversary; but it is not because the adversary is stronger, but because, as be expressly says, men have followed him and not the Creator. The Creator is exceedingly bountiful and intended to make human life easy and agreeable and death an unknown thing. He is the author warden and judge of human morality. (p. 33).

"There is also the belief that after a long time this world will fall down, all the dead will return to life, and then the World-Creator will also return and renew all things. (p. 34). in each of these religions there exists a true High God: nay, I do not hesitate to employ a more decided phrase and say: these people worship One God." (p. 129) (W. Schmidt, High Gods in North America).

"By this method we have established the weighty fact that the very first men who migrated into this continent, the first true discoverers of America, when they passed on from north-east Asia to north-west America over what is now Bering Strait, then a continuous land route, bore with them in their hearts the belief of one great God, creator of heaven and earth and man..." (W. Schmidt, High Gods in North America, p. 133).

Peoples of every land originally believed in One God.

"Look in what continent we please, we shall find the myth of a Creation or a primeval construction, of a Deluge, or a destruction and of an expected restoration." (Daniel C. Brinton, Professor of American Archaeology and Linguistics, University of Pennsylvania, in Religions of Primitive Peoples, p. 122)

CONCLUSION.

From these facts we must conclude that the Supreme Being, God, revealed His will to man when man was first created and the religions of earth are but corruptions of this original revelation.

THE BIBLE AND SCIENTIFIC FORE-
KNOWLEDGE

The Bible is not a textbook on material science. It is a textbook on religion the science of correct living. It was written hundreds of years before modern science was originated, yet it is scientifically accurate. Modern science has never disproved any statement in the Bible but has proved and demonstrated the truthfulness of hundreds of things which the Bible anticipated. The Mind which directed the writing of the Bible put into it many truths which were beyond the range of human comprehension and human knowledge at the time they were written.

SCIENTIFIC PRINCIPLES.

Herbert Spencer (1820-1903) first announced that there are only five "manifestations of the unknowable" in existence—time, force, action, space and matter and that all else is based on these fundamentals. This was hailed as a great announcement but when God had that great scientist, Moses, write the very first verse in the Bible, He said, "Moses, 3,400 years from now men will think they have discovered everything so you just put it all in Genesis 1:1 and we will begin with everything man can discover." Moses wrote: "In the beginning", time: "God", force; created", action; "the heavens", space; "and the earth", matter. Thus Moses put all five scientific fundamentals in the first verse of Genesis and they are in the same order as announced by Herbert Spencer. How could

49

Moses do this? The answer must be that God told Moses
what to write.

LIGHT BEFORE THE SUN.

All men once held with Sir Isaac Newton the idea that
light is an emanation from the sun and other luminous
bodies, but in recent years men think they have proved
that light existed before the sun. There are many theories
concerning light but all scientists are apparently agreed
that light existed before the sun was made its governor.
Since this was discovered, many pseudo-scientists have
ridiculed the "old Bible idea that light comes from the
sun." While an undergraduate in college one of my professors explained his favorite theory of light and ended
by saying, "Well, this completely upsets the old Bible
idea that light comes from the sun. In fact it just proves
that book to be out of date." "Doctor Blank, where does
the Bible say that light comes from the sun?" I asked.
"Oh, I don't know," he replied. "Everybody knows it's
there." At my insistence a Bible was brought and the professor read from the first chapter of Genesis: 'In the beginning God created the heavens and the earth and the
earth was without form and void and darkness was upon
the face of the deep; and God said, Let there be light and
there was light..." He read on to verses 17 and 1S where
God later made the sun, moon and stars to control this
light and to act as our chronometers. Seeing that Moses
was perfectly scientific, the learned doctor said, "Well,
that makes a donkey out of me." I agreed with him hearti-
ly but doubted the expediency of saying so at the time.

How did Moses know this important scientific fact thousands of years before others discovered it?

THE THREE KINGDOMS.

Scientists now teach that there are three great kingdoms mineral, vegetable and animal. This scientific division is a comparatively recent innovation. Neither the cuneiform records of Babylon and Assyria nor the hieroglyphics of Egypt reveal that the ancients knew of such a division. It is thought that Linnaeus was the first to recognize these three kingdoms and he made his announcement in A.D. 1735 while Moses wrote in 1500 B.C. In the first chapter of Genesis Moses used the first ten verses telling about the mineral material kingdom, the next nine verses telling about the vegetable kingdom and the rest of the chapter telling of the animal kingdom.

How was Moses able to make this division?

ROTUNDITY OF THE EARTH.

When the Bible was written it was universally believed that the earth was flat. It was argued that should one go too far toward the edge he would fall off. The early Grecians as well as Toscanelli, an Italian, suggested the rotundity of the earth. Columbus and others believed them. Finally, Magellan and his men sailed around the earth and thus proved it to be spherical in shape. But of the shape of the earth the Author of the Bible was not in ignorance for we read in Isaiah 40:22, "It is God that sitteth upon the circle of the earth," and in Proverbs 8:27, "He setteth a circle upon the face of the deep." We read that Christ is coming in the daytime and that He is coming at night it will be day on one side the earth and night on the other when he comes (Luke 17). That the writers of the Bible wrote of the rotundity of the earth cannot be questioned. They could have learned of this only from God. No other being in the universe could have given the information.

SUSPENSION OF THE EARTH.

The ancient Greeks and Romans were the most advanced peoples of their time, yet they believed that the earth was held in place by poles or by the neck of Atlas. Others believed that Atlas had the earth on his shoulders. Some said that the earth floated on water and should one go too far out on the sea he would surely perish. When men sailed around the earth, they discovered that it touches nothing—that nothing visible holds it in place. Then it was that the statement "...he...hangeth the earth upon nothing" (Job 28:7) was understood. The ancient book of Job is absolutely scientific. Indeed so, God told Job what to write. If not, how did he find out these things?

EMPTY SPACE IN NORTH.

Astronomers have discovered that there is a great empty space in the North. It contains no moving planets and shining stars. By turning their telescopes to the South, the East and the West, men may behold countless millions of stars invisible to the naked eye but when the telescope is set exactly to the North there is a great empty space. For this astronomers have been unable to account. They did not know until recently that there was such an empty space, yet Job declared, "He stretcheth out the North over the empty places and hangeth the earth upon nothing." (Job 26:7).

Job could not have written by guess. It must be that he wrote by inspiration of God.

MOVEMENT OF PLANETS.

The theory of the movement of the planets was first advanced by Copernicus in 1543. Calico was severely punished for believing and championing this theory, yet Job 38:31-32 clearly teaches that the planets move. The conditions mentioned in Luke 17:31-36 could be brought about only by the rotation of the earth upon its axis. The law of gravity is certainly announced in Job 26:7.

FORMATION OF STATIC ELECTRICITY.

The Greeks and Romans with all of their intellectual development thought that a thunderstorm consisted of Jupiter with a handful of thunderbolts hurling them at the earth and its peoples. Yet they might have informed themselves by reading Jeremiah 10:13, "He (God) maketh lightnings with rain." Benjamin Franklin, Thomas A. Edison and others have discovered that static electricity may be formed by condensing water, yet Jeremiah knew of this thousands of years before. How?

SCIENTIFIC PROPORTIONS OF THE ARK.

In March, 1919, the government of the United States launched its first concrete ship at San Francisco. The dimensions were 300 feet, by 50 feet, by 30 feet. This is the same proportion as the ark which Noah built. Even with all our modern development in shipbuilding we still hold to approximately the same proportions as those used by Noah in building his boat. Who taught Noah how to build ships? How did he know what proportions to make his ark?

The ark was built of gopher wood. If Noah had used some other sort of wood, the material would have perished before he finished the boat, but God, who made the laws of nature, was also the architect of the boat which Noah built.

LIGHT IS VOCAL.

The writers of the Bible knew that light is vocal. We read of "the way where light dwelleth" (Job 38:19). Job speaks not of the place where light dwells but the way. Light does not dwell in a place but is due to rapid vibrations of waves in the ether travelling at the rate of 186,000 miles each second.

Wherever there is light there is sound even if our ears are not attuned to hear it. We read that the "morning stars sang together". Light has a definite tonal value. Light, color and sound are fundamentally the same. Waves rush through space; some reach the eyes as light, some as color and some reach the ears as sound. There are rays of color (from the infrared clown) so slow and so long that our eyes cannot see them. There are rays of color (from the ultraviolet up) so short and so fast that we cannot see them. Every light and color likewise has its sound value and if our ears were turned to hear we too could hear the "morning stars sing together". Everyone is familiar with the talking film. Beside the film there is a sound track. Light is passed through this sound track and then transmuted into sound. Through its light value we hear the music and speaking of those in far off places! Job did not understand these things, yet he wrote of them. Christians, therefore, conclude that God directed Job as he wrote.

GEOGRAPHY OF THE BIBLE.

Geography is a comparatively modern science. Not many years ago the maps of much of the world were mostly blank and the mistakes in geography books must be corrected every generation. The Bible was written before the modern science of geography was ever heard of and though it abounds in geographic references, it is correct in every instance. No one has to revise it and bring it up to date. It was free of error from the beginning because the Architect of the universe is the Author of the Bible. When the Bible says, "They went up to Jerusalem" it is literally uphill. When we read "...down to Jericho" we may know it is downhill. The cities, towns, plains, deserts, hills and mountains mentioned in the Bible have been found exactly where the Bible locates them. If the Bible were a human production it would be filled with geographical errors. Since there are no such errors we conclude it is a super-human product.

PATHS OF THE SEA.

Matthew Fontaine Maury, "the pathfinder of the seas", and the founder of the science of Oceanography, was a firm believer in and a close student of the Bible. His teaching caused the Annapolis Academy to be founded and his memory is honored and respected throughout the world. On monument row in Richmond, Virginia, is a statue of the great scientist sitting with the Bible in one hand and his charts of the sea in the other. Behind him is a globe of the earth which he helped to explore.

Before Matthew Fontaine Maury lived there were no sailing lanes and no charts of the sea. One day, when he was ill, his son read to him from the eighth Psalm. He read that God put under man "...the fowls of the air, the fish of the sea, and whatsoever passeth through the paths of the sea." "Read that again," he said. Upon hearing it the second time, the venerable scientist said, "If the Word of God says there are paths in the sea, they must be there. I will find them." Within a few years he had charted the principal lanes or paths of the sea and these are followed by oceangoing vessels to this day. How did David know of these paths of the sea?

THE "SEAS" IN THEIR "PLACE".

Moses tells us in Genesis 1:10 that the "gathering together of the water called he seas". How did Moses know that there are several seas? He had not seen them. Then notice that God said, "Let the waters under the heavens be gathered together unto one place and it was so." It is literally true that the oceans are connected and thus have one bed. In the days of Moses men believed that there was one small ocean but Moses knew not only of the seas but that they have one bed. It must be that the Supreme Power of the Universe inspired Moses and guided him as he wrote

GOD QUESTIONS JOB.

After the vicissitudes and experiences of life had borne heavily upon his shoulders and he had argued with men on many questions, the ancient patriarch Job said, "Oh that I knew where I might find Him, that I might even come to His feet. I would order my cause before Him and fill my mouth with arguments. I would know the words wherewith He would say unto me." In other words Job wanted to argue with God. Many men who think they are very wise today would apparently like to argue their case with God. But first let them look at the result of Job's examination. God asked Job forty questions and Job could not answer a single one. Centuries have rolled by and the combined wisdom of the world today can answer only three or four of them. Scientists today know much that Job never dreamed of but there are forty anticipations of physical science in Job thirty-eight which are marvelous questions even for today.

God said, "Job, gird up now thy loins like a man for 1 will demand of thee, and answer thou me." God then begins the questioning: "Where wast thou when I laid the foundations of the earth?" Job could not answer. We do not know the answer today. We remember when we were small children. Parents and friends remember when we were born. Textbooks tell us something of embryology. Back of that we cannot go. We only know that life came from God. We cannot answer the question.

God then asked Job, 'Who has laid the measure thereof?" Scientists have recently pointed out that if the size of the earth were reduced it would retain less heat and would become an icy, barren waste suitable only for very low forms of life; or if its size were increased it would become a hot, tropical jungle unfit for man to live upon. (Dr. A. B. Wallace, Man's Place in the Universe, pp. 201-202). Job could not answer the question about the size of the earth. In fact no one in Job's day knew that the size of the earth had anything to do with its temperature and atmosphere.

Job was then questioned as to what holds the sea in place. He did not know. Men today have many theories but they still do not know why all the waters run into the sea and it is not full, why the sea is higher in the middle than the edges and yet does not run over.

In verse seventeen God asked Job if the gates of death had been opened to him. Job was silent. Millenniums have rolled by and we are still silent. Not one of us can pierce beyond the veil of death. The scientist confesses his inability to tell what happens beyond death and only the benevolent wisdom of the Heavenly Father gives us any idea of life "beyond the valley of the shadow of death".

God asks Job, "Hast thou entered into the treasures of the snow?" Job did not know there were any "treasures" in the snow. But Dr. Frank T. Shutt of the Canadian Department of Agriculture has recently shown that the action of snow and hail centrifuging through the air collects nitrates, free ammonia and albuminoid ammonia. These are all valuable fertilizers. He explains that an average winter's snow and hail is worth about fifteen dollars per acre to farm land.

In Job 38:34 God asks Job if he can lift up his voice to call down the rain. Job could not do it and we have not been able to do so.

Then God asks, "Cant thou send lightnings that they may go and say unto thee, here we are?" Job could not do this but we are able to do so today as we talk on the telephone and radio and send our messages by telegraph. Truly the lightning goeth and saith for us.

These questions are selected at random from Job thirty-eight. That chapter contains forty examples of scientific foreknowledge. Shall we not say that these are forty reaons for believing the Bible to be the word of God?

THE NUMBER OF THE STARS.

The ancients believed that there were only a very few stars in the heavens. In 150 B.C. Hipparchus said that there were less than three thousand. In A.D. 150 Ptolemy said there were not more than three thousand. This was considered a high estimate. After the middle ages and the invention of the telescope, men discovered that the stars are innumerable. Yet all the time Genesis 13:16, Genesis 13:5, Jeremiah 33:22 and other verses of the Bible declared that the stars of the sky are like the sands of the seashore "innumerable". How did these ancient writers know that the stars are innumerable? There can be but one answer: God told them what to write!

THE MOON A WITNESS.

Ps. 89:27 declares that the moon is a faithful witness in heaven. Now what does a witness do? He sees and testifies to others concerning that which they cannot see. The moon does exactly that. When the sun has gone down and we cannot see it shining on the other side of the earth, the moon, high up in the sky, sees and reflects the light back to us. Truly a witness! But the fact the moon sends out only reflected light was not known to men in the days of David; yet David wrote it. None would presume to suggest that David discovered it. It must be that God told David what to write.

THE SEED OF THE WOMAN.

In Genesis three and other places in the Bible we have a striking reference to the seed of the woman. This is truly a remarkable instance of scientific foreknowledge for R. C. Punnett tells us: "Few if any of the more primitive peoples seem to have attempted to define the part played by either parent in the formation of offspring....The production of offspring by men was then (the time of Aristotle) held to be similar to the production of a crop from seed. The seed came from the man, the woman provided the soil. This remained the generally accepted view for many centuries....After more than a hundred years of conflict lasting until the end of the eighteenth century, scientific men settled down to the view that each of the sexes makes a definite material contribution to the offspring produced by their joint efforts" (Mendelism, 4th edition, pp. 1-2). Thus until the end of the eighteenth century all human science and philosophy opposed the idea of the "seed of the woman". But when the facts were finally known, as is always the case, the Word of God triumphed over the theories of man.

THE VALUE OF DUST.

In Isaiah 40:12 we read that God has comprehended the dust of the earth in a measure. All people have detested dust, yet here it is spoken of along with things made for our good. Dr. Wallace in his book (op. cit). uses seven pages to tell of the value of dust (pages 205-211). He refers in the main to the fine dust of the upper atmosphere. Evidently this is what the Bible calls "the highest part of the dust of the world" (Prov. 8:26). Dr. Wallace shows that if this dust did not exist we would have less rainfall, abnormally heavy dews and a greater prevalence of fogs. He says vegetation would be greatly reduced, our blue skies would be gone and our gorgeous sunsets and sunrises would be no more. Stars would appear at midday as at midnight owing to the absence of the light reflecting elements in the air. The sun would not be reflected into houses and its light would not appear anywhere except where its rays fell directly upon the earth. Dr. Wallace suggests that it is difficult to account for this "upper dust" but that it perhaps comes from deserts and volcanoes of the earth. (Now there ought to be some red faces among those who have criticized God for making deserts and volcanoes on earth!) This authority has pointed out that without this fine dust of the upper atmosphere the earth would be uninhabitable. I simply raise this question: Why did the writers of the Bible refer to the dust as being beneficial and then why did Solomon especially point out that it is the upper dust?

ARCHAEOLOGY AND THE BIBLE

THE discovery of ancient records, written on stone, clay, parchment, paper and wax carries us back to the very time when the Bible was written. It is as if Nebuchadnezzar, Cyrus, Rameses and others mentioned in the Bible should speak from the stillness of the tomb and confirm the accuracy and credibility of the Word of God. If our Holy Bible were destroyed we might restore every institution of Christianity and much of the Book itself from the findings of archaeology.

THE CODE OF HAMMURABI.

During the months of December, 1901, and January, 1902, the great French archaeologist, M. de Morgan was making excavations in Susa, in Persia (the Shushan of Esther). He discovered a mass of black diorite eight feet high, six feet in circumference at the base and five feet at the top. Upon this monument are nearly 4,000 lines of inscriptions giving 248 laws formulated by Hammurabi, King of Babylon about 2250 B.C. He is the Amraphel of Genesis 14:1 who helped to capture Sodom and from whom Abraham wrested the spoils of battle. These laws were written in a very systematic way and show that courts and a high state of civilization existed in Babylon long before he was king. Skeptics once held that Moses could not have written the first books of the Old Testament because, they said, writing did not exist in his day. The finding of this monument shows a high state of civilization existing long before the days of Moses. There is some similarity between the laws of Moses and the laws of Hammurabi. The laws of Hammurabi, however, regard only the external act while the laws of Moses take into consideration the motives, thoughts and feelings back of every action. The laws of Moses deal with man's relationship to God as well as to his fellowman. The laws of Hammurabi deal only with man's relationship to man.

THE TEL EL-AMARNA TABLETS.

At the village of Tel el-Amarna on the Nile River about 175 miles south of Cairo, Egypt, a peasant woman found in 1887 three hundred tablets of baked clay. These tablets are now in the Louvre at Paris, France. Each tablet is covered with cuneiform inscription in the Babylonian language. They are a series of letters written about 1400 B.C. by the governors of Palestine, Phoenicia, Syria and Philistia and by the kings of Babylon and Assyria. Just as men file away important letters today for safe keeping, these letters, written in clay and baked into permanency, speak as a voice from the remote past—three thousand, five hundred years ago.

These tablets show that Palestine was a province of Egypt and had been for a long time a province of Babylon. They were written when the Hebrews were captives in Egypt and show that Palestine was in a greatly disturbed condition at the time. These letters refer to the Canaanites and to their enemies, the Hebrews. They refer to the city of Jerusalem which name was not until the finding of these tablets known to have been in use at that early date.

THE BLACK OBELISK.

In the British museum may be seen a famous monument of black marble which was cut in the reign of Shalmaneser II, King of Assyria 860-825 B.C. This stone is covered with a series of sculptured pictures showing men of many nations bringing tribute to Shalmaneser. Among them is a file of Jews who, the inscription says, came from Jehu the King of Israel (2 Kings 9, 10). This and many other monuments of Assyria describe the wars waged between Assyria and Syria and tell how Syria was a buffer state for Israel.

They show how the Assyrian defeat of Syria left Israel free to expand and thus explain many things in the history of the Northern Kingdom.

THE MOABITE STONE.

The Moabite Stone is a large slab of black basalt and is now in the Louvre at Paris. Found in ancient Moab just east of the Dead Sea, this stone was cut in the reign of Mesha, King of Moab, about 850 B.C. and is a tribute to Chemosh, the Moabite deity. It tells how Chemosh became angry with his people and allowed Omri, King of Israel, to conquer them and force them to pay tribute. It tells of the Moabites winning back their independence after the death of Ahab. The inscriptions from this stone read like a chapter from Kings. Reference is made to Jehovah, many details of the Bible are illustrated and the relations between Moab and Israel are correctly pictured.

EGYPTIAN DISCOVERIES.

Rameses II was the Pharaoh of the Egyptian bondage. His mummy has been found and every schoolboy has seen pictures of the great statue of him which lies in ancient Egypt. The city of Pithom has been discovered, the actual storehouses built by the Hebrew slaves have been found, the lower portions made of brick containing straw and the upper portions made of brick without straw. Meneptah II was the Pharaoh of the Exodus and his mummy has likewise been found. A hymn of victory addressed to him mentions Israel and the inscription tells of the death of his young son possibly in the last of the plagues. Other researches show the location of Goshen. The more the archaeologists dig in ancient Egypt, the stronger must our faith in the Old Testament become.

THE OXYRHYNCHUS PAPYRI.

These are very ancient manuscripts found about the close of the last century in a small mound near the Nile River in the Libyan desert of Egypt. Among them is a fragment of a book of sayings of Jesus evidently written about A.D. 150. These sayings are in the gospels of the Bible. Other manuscripts refer to many events which are also recorded in the Bible.

RECORD OF THE HITTITES.

The skeptics once claimed that no such nation as the Hittites ever existed since they were mentioned only in the Bible. Records of Egypt and Assyria have now been found which show that the Hittites for nearly seven centuries occupied northern Syria and southern Asia Minor and were one of the greatest nations on earth. Many ruins of Hittite buildings have been found, their rock carvings have been discovered and much of their hieroglyphic work is now being deciphered. What must be the chagrin of those who once insisted that no such nations ever existed and the joy of those who "by faith" accepted the account given in Holy Writ? Truly "the rocks and the stones cry out."

OTHER DISCOVERIES.

The ruins of Abraham's birthplace, Ur of Chaldees, have been found. Portraits of the Canaanites whom Joshua fought have been found, as well as Shishak's sculptured account of his campaign against Rehoboam. Those images bear the names of Gaza, Adullam, Adjallon, Gibeon, and Jerusalem. Tiglath-pileser's record mentions Uzziah, Ahaz, Menahem, Pekah, Hosea and five kings of Judah and Israel. We have Sargon's account of his capture of Samaria and Sennacharib's history of his invasion of Palestine mentioning King Hezekiah. Manasseh is mentioned in an Assyrian list of tributaries. Belshazzar is mentioned in the Babylonian inscriptions as being the son of Nabonidus. The excavations of Susa, Persia, have confirmed the book of Esther. The city of Nineveh has been unearthed. Hundreds of other equally interesting discoveries have been made.

CONCLUSION.

These discoveries strengthen our faith. They help us to know that the writers of the Bible "spake with authority." In the wise providence of God, the spade of the archaeologist has confounded the skeptics.

THE INFLUENCE OF THE BIBLE

A TREE is known by the fruit it bears. When we pluck the luscious fruit from the branch year after year we do not need to be convinced of the goodness of the tree we have the evidence in hand. Christians do not need to be convinced that the Bible came from God—they have seen the fruit it bears. No other book has ever had such an influence. It has always championed the right in every controversy and has never done despite to the individual who studied it. Because of its great influence, Christians believe that the Bible is a revelation from God.

MORAL INFLUENCE SPREAD ABROAD.

"Did you ever hear a man say, 'I used to steal, lie, drink, swindle, abuse my family, gamble, break up homes, beat my debts and was an immoral citizen but I was finally induced to read some books on infidelity, atheism and doubt and now I go to church, treat my family decent, pay my debts, live a moral life, try to be a good neighbor and a good citizen as the result of the influence these books had on me'? No, and you never will for the Bible is the only book that has such an influence on men." As long as the Bible has such an influence, Christians may declare with confidence, "The Bible is God's Word" and they may point with pride to its fruit.

HUMAN FREEDOM ADVANCED.

In the days of the Old Testament all nations. except the Hebrews, were built on slavery. The Hebrew nation, even when it permitted slavery surrounded it with many alleviations and held no one in servitude more than seven years. The Roman nation with a population of about one hundred and twenty-five million held more than sixty million in the basest sort of slavery. Overworked, underfed and killed at the pleasure of their owners, these slaves were indeed "without God and without hope" in the world. But lo, the Christ came and died, and from the very beginning slaves were received into the churches of Christ on the same basis as their masters. The New Testament teaches the universal Fatherhood of God and the universal brotherhood of man. Where Christianity has gone, slavery has either retreated or been destroyed. While Mohammedanism has enslaved millions, Christianity has freed millions.

THE POSITION OF WOMEN CHANGED.

In ancient times women held a degraded place among all nations except the Hebrews. In Rome a man might put his wife to death without a trial; in Greece the women who ministered to the lowest passions were highly honored. The Hebrews honored their wives and sisters. Who has not heard of Rebekah and Rachel, Ruth and Hannah, and Deborah and Esther? And time would fail us to tell of the woman who was once the virgin Mary, Mary and Martha of Bethany, Mary Magdalene, Dorcas, Lydia, Priscilla and a host of women who are highly honored in the Bible. The position of women in many eastern countries today is lower than that of the Hebrew women in

1,000 B.C. It is only in Christian lands that men and women stand side by side in doing the work which the Heavenly Father gave them to do.

WORKING MEN HELPED.

Manual labor is scorned in lands where the Bible has not gone. The Bible and its influence has given a dignity to labor which it never enjoyed before. Plato and Aristotle taught that labor was degrading. The Emperor Augustus ordered the execution of a senator who lowered his dignity by working in the garden to assist some friends. In the Old Testament every man was compelled to learn a trade. David was a shepherd boy; Amos, a farmer; Christ, a carpenter; some of the apostles, fishermen; and Paul was a tentmaker. It is a direct influence of the Bible which has permitted laborers to gain their rights and has given us cooperation instead of exploitation in industry. In view of these facts is it not disgusting to hear so-called labor leaders criticize the Bible?

CIVIL GOVERNMENT HELPED.

The greatest statesmen and lawmakers of all time have been influenced by the laws of Moses. Grecian and Roman law was influenced by Christianity. King Alfred based his famous laws on the Ten Commandments and the book of Leviticus. Blackstone exalts the influence of Christianity on our law. Sir Matthew Hale said, "Christianity is parcel of the common law." Daniel Webster said, "It seems to be a law of our human condition that Christianity and civilization can live and flourish together."

The statesmen of the world have been unable to improve the laws given by Moses more than three thousand years ago. A prominent attorney once told me, "When I am inclined to be skeptical, I read the laws given by Moses and my skepticism vanishes."

The teaching of the Bible has advanced the cause of political liberty. Christian missionaries have carried the Bible into such countries as Turkey, Persia, China, Korea and Japan, and Western civilization has followed with more liberal laws. The founders of the United State were Bible men and believed that our government should be founded upon that Book. Where the Bible is best loved and most freely read, the liberties of the people are most freely granted. When a tyrant seeks to take away the liberty of the people, one of his first acts is to take, away the Bible and attempt to close or regulate the churches. The fountainhead of Bible translation has been Geneva, Switzerland and it is no accident that it has also been the home of the World Court, the League of Nations, the World Red Cross, and the fountainhead of European emancipation. The rights of the common people are freely granted where the Bible is freely circulated.

LITERATURE INSPIRED.

English literature began with the translation of the Bible. Shakespeare filled his writings with Bible ideas and Bible phraseology. Milton and Dante borrowed freely from the Bible. Addison, Steele, Browning and Tennyson are filled with allusions to the scriptures. Sir Walter Scott called the Bible "The Book". "Pilgrim's Progress" and "The Imitation of Christ" have been perhaps the most widely read of any books among men save the Bible and they closely follow the Bible in spirit. Daniel Webster established his wonderful oratory upon the Bible and read the Bible through once a year. Most literature that is enduring, and permanent has been inspired by the Bible. What great literary productions have been inspired by the books of infidels

EDUCATION PROMOTED.

The most fundamental and necessary truths of modern scholarships are taught in the Bible. Men who believe the Bible have founded practically all our colleges and universities. Infidelity plants no schools. Ignorance is the lot of the people where the Bible has not gone. Our own system of free schools for everybody owes its origin and growth to the principles of Christianity. The Bible is counted as the outstanding influence for education by many leading educators of the world. No other book so completely sounds every depth and touches every shore of human intellect and emotion. When the question "If you were cast on a desert island and could have only one book, which would you choose?" was asked students at George Peabody College, Nashville, Tennessee, they were almost unanimous in their choice of the Bible. If one were interested only in literature what other book could he choose? If he believed in the inspiration of the Bible what other book would he choose? Well did Sir Isaac Newton say, "I count the scriptures of God to be the most sublime philosophy."

Skeptics have frequently charged that Christians seek to "bootleg" their religion into the public schools. Bootleg, indeed! The Christians have founded practically all our schools and are responsible for our school systems. The men who pay the bills have a right to say what shall be taught in their schools. If skeptics want to teach the various phases of infidelity let them build their own schools and stop "bootlegging" their doctrines into the public schools.

THE ARTS PROFOUNDLY INFLUENCED.

The influence of the Bible has enriched and exalted architecture. It has inspired not mysterious caverns, dark passageways and heathen temples trod by the feet of the few but the building of simple and beautiful buildings in every corner of the earth where the common people may go to hear the Word of Life.

The world's masterpieces of painting have been inspired by the Bible. Michelangelo's "The Bible"; da Vinci's "The Last Supper"; and Raphael's, "Sistine Madonna" together with paintings by many masters of the Madonna, the child Jesus, the crucifixion, and the ascension are all, of course, inspired by the Bible.

The Bible is filled with inspiring poetry. The Psalms are the world's noblest songs. The best of the world's music, "Samson" and "Messiah," Haydn's 'Creation", Mendelssohn's "St. Paul" and "Elijah"; the passion music of Bach—all were inspired by the Bible.

CONCLUSION.

Women have been exalted, slaves freed, working men given their rights and civil government helped; education has been promoted, literature inspired, and the best of the world's music and painting inspired all by the influence of one Book—the Bible. No other book has had such an influence. Homer and Plato did not do as much for Greece, nor Cicero and Virgil for Rome; Confucius did not do it for China nor the Koran for Arabia. The "sacred books" of the East have not even begun to bear such fruit. Why has the Bible been the fountainhead of civilization? Is it not because the eternal Spirit of God inspired the writing of its pages?

PROPHECY AND ITS FULFILLMENT

The Bible contains many remarkable prophecies which were written hundreds of years before the events described occurred and which have been accurately and minutely fulfilled. It is as if a man should now write a history of the nations which shall inhabit the earth and the wars they shall fight a thousand years hence and at that time those very things should come to pass. No stronger proof not only of the truthfulness but of the inspiration of the writers of the Bible can be found than prophecy and its fulfillment.

The criteria of true prophecy has been listed as the following: The event must be beyond the power of man to foresee; it must not be a vision of hope nor a result of fear; it must not be a scientific or political forecast. The prediction must be written before the event occurs and must be applicable to it. The language of the prophecy must be clear and the fulfillment plain. I here give some prophecies which meet all these requirements.

THE PROPHECY OF NOAH.

Noah was chosen to be the second father of the human race and from him have come all people who dwell on the earth. lie uttered a prophecy in Genesis 9:25-27 which sketches the grand outline of all history as it is given in the lives of his three sons and their descendants. These three sons of Noah were Shem, Ham and Japheth.

"Cursed be Canaan (or Ham); a servant of servants shall he be." A curse has always rested upon the nations of Hamitic origin. The Canaanites were cursed with the most abominable idolatries. Sodom and Gomorrah, Phoenicia, Tyre and Sidon were destroyed. Egypt is black with ruins, Africa is the dark continent. "Most of the slaves of the world have come from this continent. "A servant of servants shall he be" was, I think, a simple statement of what was to be rather than a judgment from heaven. At any rate, it is truth.

"Blessed of Jehovah, my God, be Shem." The descendants of Shem were blessed in that God providentially cared for them, committed the Old Testament scriptures to their care, sent the Messiah from their race and started the Kingdom of Heaven among them.

"God shall enlarge Japheth and he shall dwell in the tents of Shem; and Canaan shall be his servant." Japheth had seven sons; Shem, five; and Ham, four. The races which have come from Japheth have always ruled the largest territory and have scattered throughout the world and ruled it. In numbers, art, science, commerce and in many other ways the descendants of Japheth have been "enlarged." This prophecy is conclusive and there could be no other application.

PROPHECY CONCERNING ISHMAEL.

Abraham was not only the father of the Jewish nation but was the father of the Ishmaelites also. The prophecies concerning both Jews and Ishmaelites are abundant in the

Old Testament. Let us study the prophecy concerning Ishmael.

"Twelve princes shall he beget" (Gen. 17:20). Moses names these princes in Genesis 25 and Eusebius, writing about A.D. 350 speaks of the twelve Arabian princes of his time.

"I will multiply thy descendants exceedingly." (Genesis 16:10-12). This was God's promise to Hagar. During the time of Joseph the Ishmaelites carried on an extensive trade with Egypt. The Nabatheans, Arabs, Itureans and Saracens are Ishmaelites.

"And he will be a wild man." What better description could be given of the Arabs as they roam the desert?

"His hand will be against every man and every man's hand will be against him." The Arab has always lived by robbery and plunder. This is literally fulfilled today.

"And he shall dwell (tabernacle) in the presence of his brethren." For four thousand years the Ishmaelites have dwelt in the presence of their brethren, the descendants of Abraham and Lot. Other nations have changed but they remain as a witness for the inspiration of God's Word.

MOSES' PROPHECY CONCERNING THE JEWS (DEUT. 28).

One of the most remarkable and minute prophecies ever uttered is found in Deuteronomy 28. This prophecy was written by Moses and was fulfilled fifteen hundred years later.

This prophecy was that God would bring against the Jews a nation from afar as swift as the eagle flieth, with a fierce countenance caring for neither young nor old and speaking a language which the Jews would not understand. Moses said that this nation would besiege Jerusalem until the high and fenced walls should come down, that the people would suffer untold horrors; that they would devour human flesh and a woman would eat her own child. He prophesied that Jews would be sold into Egypt as slaves until no purchaser could be found and others would be scattered throughout the nations of the earth. He said that they would become a hiss and a byword, that they would find no rest and would be oppressed and despoiled evermore, that their plagues would be of long continuance but that God would not utterly abhor them nor utterly destroy them.

The fulfillment of each prediction of this prophecy is well known to all. In A.D. 70, a nation from afar, the Romans, speaking a strange language, besieged the city of Jerusalem. They were fierce men of battle having the swift eagle for a standard and they regarded neither old nor young. Josephus, the celebrated Jewish historian, has given a wonderful account of the destruction of Jerusalem. He says, "They did not so much as spare young children, but everyone at that time, snatching up many, and casting them down from the citadel." He says that a mother ate the flesh of her own child, that the number slain was 1,240,490 and that 99,200 were taken prisoner. These were sold into Egypt until no buyer could be found and many were slaughtered while others died of disease. Jews are now found in every nation. Where have they not been oppressed and despoiled? Since they rejected their Messiah where have they found rest? Murdered by Russian mobs under the Czar, persecuted by modern dictators and driven from nation to nation, the Jews are today living monuments to the inspiration of the Bible.

THE DESTRUCTION OF BABYLON
(ISA. 13:19-22, ISA. 14, JER. 50).

These prophecies refer to things which have happened to the ancient city of Babylon since the Old Testament was completed. The city was to be destroyed as Sodom and Gomorrah and should never be inhabited nor dwelt in from generation to generation, the Arab would not pitch his tent there nor would shepherds spend the night there with their flocks and herds. Wild beasts should dwell there, owls and doleful creatures should infest it and the cry of the bittern would be heard from its many pools of water. This city was to be plundered until the walls and foundations were overturned, the sower and harvester cut off and even the people passing by should be astonished at the desolation.

Founded in 2234 B.C., Babylon was one of the outstanding cities of ancient times. It had walls fifteen miles square, 350 feet high, and 87 feet thick, a hundred gates and towers; it had hanging gardens and splendid palaces. It was built in the fertile valley of the Euphrates and was the capitol of the great Babylonian Empire. When Babylon was at the height of her glory these prophecies were written. Twenty-five centuries have looked down upon the great city since that time. It now lies in ruins. The valley is not fertile, the farmers no longer reap and sow, the Arab and the shepherd do not live there. Pools of water now stand where once great palaces stood and the hunter pursues the wild boast and doleful creatures where once the great streets were filled with commerce. Even Volney, a skeptical historian, expressed astonishment at the desolation of the city.

THE DESTRUCTION OF NINEVEH (ZEPHANIAH AND NAHUM).

This great city was to be destroyed when its rulers were drunken, it was to be destroyed by fire, water and the armies of the enemy. It should become like a wilderness or a desert. Flocks and herds should not lie there and all who came that way would hiss and wag the head in sympathy.

Dozens of travellers have described the desolation of Nineveh. It was captured by the Medes and Persians, the floods ail fires assisting them. Diodorus, the ancient historian, tells how its rulers and defenders were too drunken to cope with the enemy. The city is now a dry wilderness though much of its charred remains have been excavated, it has not been rebuilt.

PROPHECY CONCERNING TYRE.

Located on the Mediterranean Sea between the trading centers of East and West, Tyre enjoyed much of the world's commerce. It was one of the greatest cities of ancient times and at the time of the prophecies given by Isaiah and Ezekiel was at its height.

Tyre was to be taken and destroyed by the Chaldeans. (Isa. 23:13, Ezek 26:7-11). Nebuchadnezzar was to destroy it. Its inhabitants were to pass to other lands and find no rest. After seventy years the city was to be rebuilt. Tyrian history recorded by Menander says Nebuchadnezzar besieged the city for thirteen years, the Tyrians escaping in boats to Africa, Spain and the Islands of the Mediterranean. Finding no rest, they returned seventy years later and rebuilt the city.

Tyre was to be taken and destroyed the second time. (Isa. 23:6, Ezek. 27:32, Zech. 9:3-4). The ruins of old Tyre were to be cast into the sea, fire and sword were to destroy the new city and the inhabitants were to be sold into slavery. This prophecy was fulfilled when Alexander the Great destroyed the city. New Tyre was built off the shore on an island in the sea. Alexander used the ruins and soil of the Old Tyre to build a causeway, marched into the city and destroyed it. Fifteen thousand were saved and thirty thousand were sold into slavery.

The people of Tyre were to forsake idolatry and accept the true word of God. (Ps. 45:12, Zech. 9:1-7, Isa. 23:18). Multitudes came from Tyre and the sea coast to hear Jesus. Jesus preached in the cities nearby and Paul found a church there and tarried seven days. Eusebius says these prophecies were fulfilled in his day.

This city was to be finally destroyed and become a place where fishermen would spread their nets. "Thus sayeth the Lord, Behold I bring against thee, O Tyrus, and I will cause many nations to come up against thee, as the sea causeth her waves to come up. And they shall destroy the walls of Tyrus and break down her towers; I will also scrape her dust from her, and make her top like a rock. It shall be a place for the spreading of nets in the midst of the sea; for I have spoken it, saith the Lord." (Ezekiel 26:3). "Thou shalt be no more." (Ver. 14).

This is the present condition of Tyre. Brother J. W. McGarvey in his "Lands of the Bible" gives a striking description of this desolation. Another traveller long ago wrote, "This city, standing in the sea, upon a peninsula, promises at a distance, something magnificent. But when you come to it you find no similitude of that glory for which it was once so renowned in the ancient times. On the north side is an old broken Turkish garrison, besides which you see nothing but a mere Babel of broken wall, pillars, vaults, etc., there being not so much as one entire house left; its present inhabitants are poor wretches, harboring themselves in the vaults and subsisting chiefly upon fishing, who seem to be preserved in this place by divine Providence, as a visible argument how God fulfilled his word concerning Tyre, viz., that it should be 'as the top of a rock, a place for fishers to dry their nets on'."

PROPHECY CONCERNING EGYPT.

The ancient prophets said that Egypt would become desolate in the midst of desolation; that there would no longer be a prince of Egypt but that the country would be ruled by strangers. It was to become a base kingdom but idolatry was to be destroyed and the country finally redeemed. (Isa. 19:19-25, Ezekiel 29:3-20).

This country has literally become desolate. The valley of the Nile is strewn with the monuments of departed glory. The pyramids, temples, and deserted cities of ancient Egypt are silent witnesses to the inspiration of the prophets. Since 350 B. C. Egypt has been ruled and oppressed by the Persians, the Greeks, the Romans, the Saracens, the Mamelukes and the Turks. In later years it has been ruled by England. It became a base kingdom—its people, its rulers, its government and its barbarism. Yet idolatry was destroyed by the false prophet (Mohammedanism) as predicted. There are signs that Egypt is now waking from her long sleep and she may yet hold an important place in the history of the world.

THE UNIVERSAL EMPIRES OF THE EARTH.

The second chapter of Daniel predicts that there would be five and only five universal, world-wide empires. These were to be the Babylonians, the Medo-Persian, the Grecian, and Roman and the Kingdom of Christ. The fulfillment of these prophecies is verified in every outline of the history of the great empires of the world. Daniel said Babylon was represented by the head of gold on the great image which he saw showing that it was first and lasted longer than any of the other kingdoms. The Medo-Persian Empire was inferior to Babylon and was represented by the breast and arms of silver. These two arms represented Media and Persia. This empire was rich in silver. The Grecian Empire was represented by brass.

The soldiers of Alexander the Great were called the brazen-coated Greeks. The Roman Empire was represented first in its two divisions, then in its ten divisions, by the iron legs and the feet of iron mixed with clay. The kingdom of Christ is represented by the little stone cut out of the mountain without hands showing that it was a divine institution and not a political kingdom. The civilized world is now so large and so divided that there could scarcely be another world-wide empire, hence Daniel was correct in his outline of the empires of the world.

THE RISE OF MOHAMMEDANISM.

The rise of the false prophet, Mohammed, and his system of religion is clearly foretold by Daniel in chapter seven. He sees two animals on the banks of the river Ulai. The ram represents the Persian power and the he-goat, with a horn between his eyes, represents the Grecian power under Alexander the Great. The single horn is broken off and four others come in its place. This represents the death of Alexander the Great and the four-fold division of his kingdom into Greece, Thrace, Syria, and Egypt. Out of one of these horns grew the little horn representing the Mahometan power. These points of history are well known. The items of prophecy were that it should rise in a division of Alexander's empire after Greece had lost her power, that it should be peculiar in cunning and skill. It was to make war on the Holy Land and be broken without hands. All this exactly fits the rise of Mohammedanism and its continual war on Christianity.

Conclusion.

These prophecies are examples from the Sacred Scriptures and scarcely "touch the hem of the garment". The history of dozens of nations and cities may be found in prophecy in the Old Testament. The prophecies given are clear and hundreds of years intervene between the prophecy and its fulfillment. In every case the agreement is perfect. The divisions of the human race, the fate of specific peoples, the rise and fall of cities and the course of universal empire are predicted with startling clearness. Chance, mathematical calculation, and ingenious interpretation cannot account for these remarkable prophecies and their fulfillment. "Holy men of God spake as they were moved by the Holy Spirit."

This outline of prophecy was used half a century ago by H. W. EVEREST.

THE MESSIANIC PROPHECIES

A complete history of the life of Christ was written more than eight hundred years before he was born. This detailed account of His life could not have been written in advance unless the Creator of the universe had guided those who wrote.

COMING OF MESSIAH FORETOLD.

The first promise of the coming of Christ was made after the first sin when God said to Satan, "I will put enmity between thee and the woman, and between thy seed and her seed; it shall bruise thy head, and thou shalt bruise his heel." The "Seed of the woman" is Christ and the serpent is the devil. Satan was to inflict a wound but not a fatal one—Christ would be crucified but would rise from the dead. He was to bruise Satan's head. The promise to Abraham (Gen. 12:3) "In thee shall all families of the earth be blessed" refers to the coming of Christ. God promised David (Jer. 23:5-6) "Behold, the days come, saith the Lord, that I will raise up unto David a righteous Branch, and a King shall reign and prosper, and shall execute justice and judgment on the earth. In his days Judah shall be saved and Israel shall dwell safely; and this is the name whereby he shall be called, The Lord our Righteousness."

Isaiah (9:6) prophesied, "For unto us a child is born, unto us a son is given; and the government shall be upon his shoulders; and his name shall be called Wonderful, Counsellor, the Mighty God, the Everlasting Father, the

Prince of Peace." These titles could be applied only to Christ. Malachi closes the Old Testament with a promise of the Lord's coming.

Hundreds of Old Testament prophecies relate to the coming of Christ. These are sufficient to show that in every age the promise of His coming was kept alive in the heart of man.

TIME OF CHRIST'S COMING FORETOLD.

Christ was to come in the "last days". (Isa. 2:2, Joel 2:28). Peter quotes this as being fulfilled in the second chapter of Acts. He was to come during the fourth universal empire — the Roman Empire. (Daniel 2:44). "And it came to pass in those days there went out a decree from Caesar Augustus that all the world should be taxed." (Lk. 2:1). "Now in the fifteenth year of the reign of Tiberius Caesar, Pontius Pilate being governor of Judea, and Herod being tetrarch of Galilee...Annas and Caiaphas being high priests..." Thus the coming of Christ and of John, His harbinger, was during the days of the Roman Empire.

Christ was to come while the temple was yet standing. "...and the Lord whom ye seek shall suddenly come to His temple." (Mal. 3:1). "I will fill this house with glory saith the Lord." (Hag. 2:7). Christ often went into the temple. Soon after he left the earth the temple was destroyed.

Christ was to come before Judah ceased to be a distinct and ruling tribe. "The sceptre shall not depart from Judah nor a lawgiver from between his feet, until Shiloh come;

and unto him shall the gathering of the people be." (Gen. 49:10). The "sceptre" was the standard of the tribe of Judah and a symbol of the tribe itself. It signifies a ruler and a lawgiver. This prophecy simply means that before Judah lost its tribal distinctness and rulership the Christ would come. Only one Jewish tribe remained distinct in the days of Christ and this still maintained a high priest or ruler. In the destruction of Jerusalem, A. D. 70, both tribe and priest disappeared. Today no Jew knows from what tribe he comes.

The very year of Christ's coming is foretold by Daniel in Daniel 9:25, "Know therefore and understand that from the going forth of the commandment to restore and build Jerusalem unto the Messiah the Prince, shall be seven weeks, threescore and two weeks." According to the usage of Daniel, a day represents a year. The decree for rebuilding Jerusalem was in 457 B.C. Beginning at this time the 483 years bring us down to the personal ministry of Christ.

Just as the astronomer predicts the eclipse of the sun and it comes to pass, so the prophets told the very time Christ would come and, lo, He appeared!

PLACE OF CHRIST'S BIRTH FORETOLD.

It was predicted that Christ would be born in "Bethlehem Ephratah" and that his "goings forth have been from of old, from everlasting." (Micah 5:2). This statement is clear. Christ was born in Bethlehem Ephraith—not Bethlehem in Galilee. "Now Jesus was born in Bethlehem of Judea." (Matt. 2:1). Joseph and Mary lived in Galilee, yet when Christ was born they were in the south of Palestine in Bethlehem of Judea just as the prophet predicted

CHRIST'S LINEAGE FORETOLD.

He was to be a descendant of Abraham. (Gen. 12:1-3, Gal. 3:16). And of Isaac (Gen. 21:12, Heb. 11:18) and David (Jer. 23:5, Acts 13:23, Rom. 1:3).

Christ was to be of the tribe of Judah. Gen. 49:10 says that "Shiloh" would come from this tribe and Heb. 7:14 says, "it is evident that our Lord sprang out of Judah."

Christ was to derive His human nature from the woman and his divine nature from God. (Gen. 3:15, Gal. 4:4, Lk. 1:35).

CHRIST'S CHARACTER FORETOLD.

The prophets said that Christ would be meek and lowly, a man of sorrows, unpopular, persecuted; that He would be a King and desired of all people. Only in Christ do we have contradictory features manifested. He was to love righteousness, gentleness and tenderness. He was to obey the Father in all things. It was predicted that He would save others but not Himself. All these things were true in every respect.

EVENTS IN CHRIST'S LIFE FORETOLD.

It was. divinely prophesied that a harbinger would go before Christ to prepare the way for Him. He was to go in the power and spirit of Elijah. This, of course, refers to

John the Baptist who prepared the way for Christ. (Mal. 3:1, Lk. 1:17, Isa. 40:3, Matt. 17:10-13).

The Messiah was to confirm His message with miracles of healing the blind, deaf and lame. (Isa. 35:5-6). This He did abundantly during the whole of His personal ministry.

He was to be rejected by His brethren and hated by the Jews. (Ps. 69:8, Jno. 1:11, Jno. 15:24).

Christ was forsaken by His disciples (Zech. 13:7, Matt. 26:31) and sold for thirty pieces of silver. (Zech. 11:12, Matt. 26:15).

Hundreds of other events in the life of Christ have been foretold but these are sufficient to show that the prophets wrote a complete history of His life before He was born.

CRUCIFIXION AND BURIAL FORETOLD.

Christ was to die under a judicial sentence and not at the hands of a mob. "He was taken from prison and from judgment and who shall declare his generation for he was cut off out of the land of the living." (Isa. 53:8). Though Christ did not receive a just trial yet He died under a judicial sentence.

He was to die by crucifixion. "He shall be cut off out of the Land of the living" seems to indicate a violent death. "For dogs have encompassed me: the assembly of the wicked have enclosed me: they pierced my hands and feet." (Ps. 22:16). Only in crucifixion were the hands and feet pierced.

He was to be scourged before His crucifixion. (Isa. 50:6). Soldiers were to gamble for His Clothing. (Ps. 22:18). "Then when the soldiers had crucified Jesus, they took His garments and made four parts, to every soldier a part; now the coat was without seam, woven from the top throughout. They said among themselves, let us not rend it but cast lots for it, whose it shall be." (Jno. 19:23-24).

Christ was to perish among His enemies and in the midst of cruel mockings. (Ps. 22:6-11). His side was to be pierced. (Zech. 12:10, Jno. 19:34).

Those who killed Christ expected to bury Him with the wicked criminals but the prophet had written, "And he made His grave with the wicked and with the rich in his death," hence we see Joseph of arimathea, a rich man begging the body of Jesus that he might bury it in his new made tomb. (Isa. 53:9, Matt. 27:57-60). Nicodemus, another rich man, helped to embalm the body. He brought about a hundred pounds of myrrh and aloes and linen clothes. Surely it was intended to bury Jesus with the paupers and criminals but He was "with the rich in His death"!

RESURRECTION, ASCENSION, AND
CORONATION PREDICTED.

Christ was to rise from the dead. The Old Testament scripture foretold this and the disciples of Christ heard

Him predict it when He was with them. No other religious teacher ever risked His claims on His own resurrection from the dead. (Isa. 53:10, 11, Matt. 20:18-19, Acts 2:29-32).

The ascension of Christ was foretold. He was to conquer death and ascend on high. (Ps. 68:18). This He did. Picture the solemn occasion as Jesus stands on the hilltop of Judea and bids goodbye to His disciples. He leaves upon them the burden of spreading His kingdom and goes with the clouds toward that home from whence He came. As He draws near heaven there is great rejoicing. A Son who has been gone from home for thirty-three years is returning. He has been to earth, suffered, died and finished the work His Father gave Him to do. Now He returns and angels meet Him singing, "Lift up ye gates and be ye lift up ye everlasting doors and the King of glory shall come in." Christ is ushered into the presence of God. He is crowned Lord of Lords and King of Kings. He is seated on David's throne and there is given Him "dominion and glory and a kingdom, that all peoples, nations and languages should serve Him: His dominion is an everlasting dominion which shall not pass away, and His kingdom that which shall not be destroyed." (Acts 1:9, Eph. 4:8, Dan. 7:13-14, Ps. 24:7-10).

CONCLUSION.

All these prophecies were written more than five hundred years before the death of Christ. They constitute a storehouse of information to strengthen our faith and to convict the gainsayer. They cannot be the result of fortunate guessing or blind chance. The hundreds of prophecies in the Old Testament concerning the Christ and their minute fulfillment as recorded in the New Testament simply prove to the candid and thoughtful person that the Bible is the inspired Word of God.

PROOF FROM SECULAR WRITERS

CHRISTIAN WRITERS

AN UNBROKEN Chain of secular writers who have quoted from the New Testament and attributed its books to their reputed authors reaches from the present back to the apostolic age. The integrity and genuineness of the New Testament does not depend upon these secular writers but if the entire New Testament were destroyed we would be abundantly able to reproduce every verse from the writings of these early writers commonly called "church fathers".

THE FIRST CENTURY

Ignatius

Ignatius, Bishop of Antioch, was born about A.D. 37 and was martyred at Rome in 108: He served as Bishop of Antioch until 95. Of his works we have seven short epistles which are conceded to be genuine. These contain nine-teen quotations from the New Testament. When Ignatius was being taken to Rome to be put to death he was permitted to preach to Christians along the way. Just before his death he wrote to the church at Ephesus thanking them for their kindness to him. He mentions that Onesimus comforted him in prison as he had previously comforted Paul and others and quotes from Paul's letter to the Ephesians. His letters to Polycarp, to the church at Smyrna and to the church at Philadelphia also contain quotations from the New Testament.

Barnabas.

Barnabas, the travelling companion of the apostle Paul, wrote a famed work usually called "The Epistle of Barnabas". This work was completed about A.D. 98. The genuineness of this epistle was questioned until 1859 when Dr. Tischendorf found a complete copy of the Greek text in the Convent of St. Catherine. Since that time the critics have been silent. In this epistle Barnabas quotes Jno. 3:14, Jno. 6:58, Jno. 8:58 and notably Matt. 22:14 which is introduced with the phrase "It is written". He refers to Matt. 9:13, Matt 20:16, Acts 4:32 and at least ten or twelve other passages from the New Testament. He writes a passage which is strikingly similar to Romans 6:1-4. He refers to the Judaising tendency of the time, the worship of the Lord's Day, the commandment of baptism, and many other facts of the New Testament.

Polycarp.

Polycarp was born prior to A.D. 70 and was martyred in A.D. 155. When called upon to recant his faith in the Lord Jesus or be put to death this venerable Christian said, "Eighty-six years have I served Him, and He never did me any injury; how then can I blaspheme my King and Savior?" Polycarp was a student and convert of the Apostle John. He wrote a long letter to the church at Philippi which is genuine beyond all question. He refers by name to Paul's letter to the same church and quotes forty times from eleven other New Testament books.

Clement of Rome.

Clement of Rome died about A.D. 120. He wrote several epistles of which the one to the Christians at Corinth, written about A.D. 80, shows him to have been familiar with the writings of Peter and Paul and John's gospel. He alludes to many things found in the Hebrew epistle. He quotes thirty-one times from seventeen books of the New Testament.

Hermas.

The "Shepherd of Hermas" is a very ancient document written about the close of the first century. It is sad to contain twenty-three quotations from fourteen books of the New Testament.

SECOND CENTURY

Irenaeus.

Irenaeus was born at Smyrna and lived between 120 and 202. He was a pupil of Polycarp and became Bishop of Lyons in 178. He was martyred for his defense of the gospel and his five books "Against Heresies" remain to this day. He quotes from every book of the New Testament save one and these quotations in all number 767.

Justin Martyr.

Justin, the martyr, was born at Neapolis about the close of the first century and was put to death at Rome under Marcus Aurelius in 167. He was an outstanding student of Philosophy and Greek and was so well known that the manner of his death has become a part of his name. He was a copious writer and many of his works are preserved. The outstanding are two Apologies and a Dialogue with Trypho, a Jew. He quotes about 125 times from Matthew, Mark, Luke, John and other New Testament books. In giving an account of the last supper he says, "The Apostles, in the Memoirs composed by them, which are called Gospels, have thus informed us." "On the day which is called Sunday we all, whether dwelling in cities or in the country, assemble together; when the Memoirs of the Apostles or the writings of the Prophets are read, as long as time permits." Justin gave the following as an outline of Christian worship: Scripture lesson from the New Testament, Sermon, Prayer with the congregation standing, the offering, Holy Communion celebrated every Sunday. "He being dead yet speaketh".

Tertullian.

Tertullian lived in Carthage between 160 and 220. He was a pagan and a Roman lawyer. Later he became a Christian and a defender of the faith. He recognizes the four gospels as written by Matthew, Mark, Luke and John. His greatest work is "Against Marcion". He gives 1,802 long quotations from twenty-four books of the New Testament. For himself and for Christians of all ages he gives strong evidence of the existence, genuineness and credibility of these books.

Clement of Alexandria.

Clement of Alexandria was born about 160 and died in 220. He was a man of great ability and much learning. He calls the scriptures divinely inspired and says that the existence of one God is proved by the Law, the Prophets and the "blessed Gospels". In his works he quotes so much from the Bible that he refers to every book in the Old Testament except Ruth and the Song of Solomon and all books in the New Testament save James, Philemon and Second Peter. He refers to Matthew, Mark, Luke and John and names them in that order. In all nearly four hundred quotations from the New Testament are found in the writings of Clement of Alexandria.

Papias.

Papias was a contemporary of the disciples of the Apostles and was Bishop of Hierapolis in Phrygia. He wrote a book on Christ's teaching in which he tells how Mark wrote his gospel from information given him by Peter and how Matthew at first wrote in Hebrew and the people translated it as best they could.

Basilides.

Basilides lived about 130 and wrote a 24-volume commentary on the gospels. He quotes also Rom. 8:22 and 2 Cor. 12:4 and alludes to Romans, Ephesians, Colossians, I Timothy and I Peter.

THIRD CENTURY

Origen of Egypt.

Origen of Alexandria, Egypt, was a son of Christian parents and trained in the faith from childhood. He was born in 186 and died in 253. His father was martyred when

Origen was sixteen years old and from that day forward Origen wrote a steady stream of books on the Christian religion. Ambrosius, a wealthy man, was converted through his teaching and put his entire fortune at the disposal of Origen. With about thirty clerks and shorthand writers, Origen wrote commentaries on every book of the New Testament and most books of the Old Testament. He arranged in six parallel columns the whole Bible consisting of the six outstanding texts and versions of his day. His books contain thousands of quotations from all parts of the Bible. When death stilled his pen in A.D. 253 he had completed, perhaps, the greatest amount of work ever done by one man in defense of the Christian religion against paganism.

Cyprian and others.

Cyprian was Bishop of Carthage and wrote from 230 to 256. He wrote a commentary on 2 Timothy and makes more than fifty quotations from various books of the New Testament. Hippolytus wrote many books near the beginning of the third century. He urged Christians to build on the entire New Testament and not on isolated texts. Athanasius, Basil the Great, Ammonius and others wrote many volumes in defense of the New Testament in the third century.

FOURTH CENTURY

Augustine and Eusebius together with a score of other writers wrote so much during the fourth century that the entire Bible might, if lost, be restored from their writings.

Eusebius was born in Palestine about 260. He was Bishop of Caesarea and wrote an Ecclesiastical History in ten volumes. When he wrote there were only four gospels: Matthew, Mark, Luke and John. He says these gospels together with the other books of the New Testament were accepted by the churches everywhere as being genuine and authentic.

It is useless to cite authors who refer to the Bible since the fourth century. Since that time the whole Bible has taken such a part in both civil and religious affairs that its existence and wide distribution would not be questioned by any sane man.

CONCLUSION.

We conclude that the New Testament if lost could be restored from the writings of the "church fathers" in any century back to the first one; that the New Testament as we now have it has existed and been accepted as genuine and authentic in every century since the apostles lived. Many of us have heard some of our college professors parade before their classes and say, "The New Testament was not written until the third or fourth century". This study leads us to conclude that they were either woefully ignorant or willfully dishonest.

NON-CHRISTIAN WRITERS

By a plain and independent path—that of non-Christians we are able to trace our Bible back to the days of the Apostles and thus establish its genuineness. Indeed, if all the Bible were destroyed and all the writings of the believers should perish we would be able to restore the Bible from the quotations found in the writings of its enemies.

Josephus.

Josephus, the celebrated historian, was born at Jerusalem four years after the ascension of Jesus. He was present at the destruction of Jerusalem in A.D. 70 and wrote his history of that destruction shortly afterward. He finished his history of the Jews near the close of the first century Josephus refers to the Pharisees, Sadducees and Herodians and makes several references to John the Baptist. His account of the death of Herod is similar to that given in Luke 12 and his reference to Felix, Drusilla and Bernice confirm the account. From his "Jewish Antiquities." 28, chapter 3, section 3, we quote, "Now there was, about this time, Jesus, a wise man, if it be lawful to call him man; for he performed many wonderful works. He was a teacher of such men as received the truth with pleasure. He drew over to him many of the Jews and also of the Gentiles. This was the Christ. And when Pilate, at the instigation of the principal men among us, had condemned him to the cross, those who had loved him from the first did not cease to adhere to him. For he appeared to them alive the third day, the divine prophets having foretold these and ten thousand other wonderful things concerning him. And the tribe of Christians so named for him subsists to this time." Modern critics have constantly argued that this passage is an interpolation, but it is found in all the Josephus manuscripts and is written in the style of the Jewish historian.

Tacitus.

Tacitus, the masterly Roman historian, was born in A. D. 59, twenty-five years after the crucifixion, he wrote that Nero charged Christians with his own crime of burning Rome. He also says that Christ was put to death by Pilate as a malefactor, that Christianity arose in Judea, took its name from Christ and spread from there to Rome. He says that there was a great multitude of Christians in Rome and that they were made to endure horrible sufferings; that they were torn to pieces by animals, crucified and burned to death. This account is confirmed by many other writers and even Gibbon admits that it is the truth.

Suetonius.

This historian was born about A.D. 70 and in his work on the life of Claudius, who reigned from A.D. 41 to 54, he says that Claudius "banished the Jews from Rome who were making disturbances, Christus (a heathen name Christ) being their leader." This fact is referred to in Acts 18:2, the emperor not making the proper distinction between Jews and Christians.

Pliny.

Pliny was governor of Pontus and Bithynia and a contemporary of Tacitus. From his letter to the emperor we learn that Christ was a real person, that He was worshipped as divine, that His followers were accustomed to meet on a stated day for worship, that there were many Christians and they were terribly persecuted by the Roman authorities.

Hegesippus.

Hegesippus in writing of Domitian who reigned between 81 and 96 says, "There were at that time yet remaining of the kindred of Christ the grandsons of Jude, who was called his brother according to the flesh. These some accused as being of the race of David, and Evocatus brought them before Domitianus Caesar; for he, too, was afraid of the coming of Christ, as well as Herod." Gibbon accepts this and puts it into his history.

Lucian.

Lucian, the Grecian "Mark Twain" who was born in A.D. 124, pictured the unwavering faith and calmness of Christians when being tried for their faith.

Edicts of Roman Emperors.

The edicts of the Roman emperors from Nero to Constantine commanding the persecution of Christians are governmental recognition of Christianity as existing and causing commotion. They bear testimony to its rapid spread, the purity of its morals and the heroic endurance of its followers.

Porphyry.

Porphyry wrote about A.D. 270. He was a severe critic of Christianity and made many plain references to Matthew, Mark, Acts and Galatians. He did not question the genuineness of any New Testament book though he did attack the genuineness of Daniel in the Old Testament.

Celsus.

Celsus wrote about 75 years after the death of John the apostle. He gives more than eighty quotations from the New Testament.

Hierocles.

Hierocles was President of Bithynia, a cruel persecutor and a sarcastic writer. He wrote in A.D. 303 in criticism of the "internal flaws" of the New Testament and mentioned six of the eight authors of the Book.

Julian.

In 361 the Emperor Julian composed his work against Christianity. He united learning, power and zeal in attacking the New Testament. He bore witness to the genuineness of the gospels and Acts of Apostles. He concedes their early date and accepts them as being written by their reputed authors. He quotes from Romans, Corinthians and Galatians.

CONCLUSION.

These bitter enemies are made to bear unwilling but deci-sive testimony to the existence of the Bible in all ages since the first century and to the authorship of the very books they criticized. Someone has well said, "The more the truth is rubbed, the brighter it will shine."

THE OTHER SACRED BOOKS

Are there not other sacred books in the world? How do we know that our Bible is the truth and these books are false? Could it not be that we are wrong and they are right? Are not all sacred books on the same level anyway?" These and similar questions are asked sometimes by honest inquirers and many times by those who desire with this quibble to evade the force of what is known to be the truth. There are no sacred books which may be compared with the Bible. There are many, however, which may be contrasted with it.

THE HINDU WRITINGS.

Hinduism arose in Northern India about 2,000 years before Christ and has produced a steady stream of literature from then until now. Its principal writings are: The Veda (or Rig-Veda) consisting of 1,028 hymns, teaching a simple and nearly monotheistic worship of nature; the Brahmas, which is a ritualistic enlargement of the Veda, formed to support the caste system and its arrogant exaltation of the priesthood; the Upanishads, a philosophic unfolding of the Veda; the Laws of Manti, a complete setting forth of the Hindu system; the Darsanas, or writings of the six philosophic sects of Hinduism—one being the worship of the very words of the Veda, another pantheism, etc. The epic poems, Ramayana and Mahabharta, are now included in Hindu sacred scripture and the hero of each poem is deified.

The real authors of these Hindu writings are unknown but they were arranged in their present form about 1,000 B.C. They contain absurdities of the worst sort as for example the idea that Brahma, the "universal spirit", hatched out of a golden egg and from it formed heaven and earth, or that, Mahabharta, one of their gods, has sixteen thousand wives and one hundred and eighty thousand children.

Of the teaching of the Veda this is the sum: "Your diseased condition proceeds from ignorance—ignorance that your real nature is one with God's nature; that your soul is part of the one self-existent soul of the universe—is a portion of the one infinite Essence (Brahman) which delights in infinite manifestations of itself, yet imposes a kind of self-ignorance on every separate soul proceeding out of itself. Your only cure is to get self-knowledge; but, to gain it, you will go through countless penances, fastings, pilgrimages, purifications, in this life; and, after this life, to expiate your evil deeds in eight million, four hundred thousand forms of subsequent existences—in men, animals, and even plants. Then, at the end of long ages of discipline, you will become fit for reunion with the one self-existent Being whence you proceeded, and with whom you are really identified!" (Sir M. Monier-Williams).

Snakes, antelopes, cows, monkeys and other animals are worshipped in India. Indeed, they are the reincarnations of human beings. Snakes may bite and kill and monkeys may strip bare the fields without fear of molestation. The deadly cobra is especially venerated. All travellers report the sacred cows to be a nuisance. This is but the growth of that background of darkness and superstition which Hinduism has brought. The foulest forms of obscenity are practiced in imitation of like deeds ascribed to their deities. There is no brotherhood of man in India. The goal of each individual is annihilation. Womanhood is degraded and child widows are the pity of the world. Until outside influence stayed its hand, Hinduism murdered female infants and burned widows on the funeral pyre of their husbands. There is scarcely anything barbarous which cannot truthfully be said about Hinduism. About the only good which can be found is the recognition that a Supreme Power exists and that He can reveal Himself to man. There is no evidence that the writings of Hinduism are inspired nor do they in any way compare with our Holy Bible.

THE ZEND-AVESTA OF THE ZOROASTRIANS.

Zoroaster, celebrated sage of ancient Persia, was the supposed founder of the religion embodied in the Zend-Avesta. This religion is practically gone from its Persian home but lives with the Parsees of India who say that Zoroaster lived about 500 B.C. If he lived at all he probably lived much earlier. His very existence is a matter of doubt. Some of the oldest writings of the Zend-Avesta are said to date from 700 or 800 B.C. Originally there were about twenty-one books which flourished in Persia, India, Media and nearby regions. From the time of Alexander the Great these declined until now only about thirty or forty hymns remain. There are, perhaps, not more than 100,000 adherents of this religion remaining today.

The Zoroastrians worship fire, water, the sun, the moon, and the trees. They teach that there is a perpetual conflict between good and evil, life and death, and a countless number of demons and angels contending for the mastery of the world. The faithful are said to pass over the "narrowed bridge" and "encouraged by their consciences" to enjoy unending bliss while the unfaithful fall off the bridge and are lost. Countless superstitions are encouraged. The whole religion is simply a "heap of rubbish" which indicates that once the founders of the religion may have had an idea of the truth but which shows that the depravity and superstition of man has corrupted it.

THE CONFUCIAN TEXTS.

Confucius, the Chinese philosopher, was born in 551 B.C. and lived until he was 72 years of age. He began to teach ancient literature, history and the principles of human duty when he was twenty-one years old. He compiled—not originated—the confucian texts in his old age and commentaries have been added by Mencius and other sages,

Confucius claimed to be only a man. His writings give a system of morality but can hardly be called a religion. He stated the golden rule in a negative form, viz., "What you do not wish done to yourself, do not do to others," but said he was unable to obey that rule. Confucius was never actually deified until the twentieth century but sacrifices and offerings have been made to him for many centuries. There is a Confucian temple in every district of China and most Chinese are Confucians. (In fact, most Chinese are adherents of two or three religions). The idea

of God is absent from the writings of Confucius, worship
of emperor takes the place of God, women are placed in
an inferior sphere, seven grounds for divorce are listed
and polygamy is countenanced. A father is permitted to
become a tyrant over his child. One of the tenets of Confucius—though seldom referred to—permits one to tell
lies on certain occasions. This idea has left its mark on
the 400,000,000 people of China, many of whom put it
into practice. The system of Confucius, while it contains
some good moral teaching, offers no hope beyond the
grave and prevents no superstition or idolatry in this life.

THE BUDDHIST WRITINGS.

Gautama (the Buddha) lived about 500 B.C. He was a
member of a small military tribe in India but was of Persian origin. Early in life he claimed to have discovered
that life offers nothing but vexation and separated himself from his family and began a life of lonely contempla-
tion. While sitting under a tree in Bengal he claims to
have attained perfect wisdom by extinction of all desires
and passions both good and bad. Buddhists think the spot
where this tree stood is the center of the earth.

Buddha "the enlightened one" himself wrote nothing but
his teaching spread among the Mongolian races in much
of India, China, Asia and Japan. His followers committed
his teaching to writing and these writings are known as
the "Tripitka" or triple collection because there are three
divisions—Vimaya, containing rules of discipline; Sutra,
containing precepts and rules of moral conduct; and Ab-
bidharma, containing largely explanations of the precepts.

Buddha taught that all existence is hopeless misery. That this misery can be extinguished by going out of existence. This going out of existence is "Nirvana" and may be attained by right belief, right speech, right means of livelihood, right memory, right aspiration, right conduct, right endeavor and right meditation. A translation of Buddha's first sermon is this: "Birth is suffering. Decay is suffering. Illness is suffering. Death is suffering. Presence of objects we hate is suffering. Separation from objects we love is suffering. Not to obtain what we desire is suffering. Clinging to existence is suffering. Complete cessation of thirst or of craving for existence is cessation of suffering." No one can write a more pessimistic speech!

Death is no escape from suffering according to Buddha as the spirit simply passes into a higher or lower form of existence as a clod of dirt, a toad, a plant, an animal, a slave, a woman, or a god, depending on the merit or demerit of the previous existence. The Buddha is said to have gone through every conceivable form of existence in water, in the air, in hell, on earth and in heaven. Buddha taught that finally one might be annihilated but that only three or four persons had ever attained this

Buddhism teaches that a soul set on attaining Nirvana should not converse with a female and "if his mother have fallen into a river, and be drowning, he shall not give her his hand to help her out, but if there be a pole at hand he may reach that to her; but if not, she must drown." Women are dishonored, marriage is scorned. Some passages in the Buddhist scriptures are so vile that they cannot be translated and printed in English.

While Buddhism has been enslaving the minds of millions with superstition and impressing them with the futility of existence, Christianity has been spreading hope and cheer and lifting people up to a higher plane of life in this present world and offering eternal late in the world to come.

The Buddhists have seen the rapidity with which Christianity has spread throughout the earth and have attributed this to the miracles which Jesus performed and to his miraculous birth. Consequently, since the sixth century they have been busy inventing miracles which they claim Buddha performed and they have now begun to claim that Buddha was born of a virgin!

THE KORAN, CODE OF ISLAM OR MOHAMMEDANISM.

Mohammed, the celebrated false prophet of Arabia, was born in A.D. 570. He claimed to teach his followers the resignation to the will of God and that he was a successor to Abraham, Moses and Christ and, of course, greater than any of them. When a child he suffered from epileptic fits and all through his life was subject to hysteria. His mind contained a strange mixture of truth and error and he sought to unite Christianity, Judaism and heathenism into one religion.

Mohammed claimed to have received the "revelations in the Koran" from God. He said, "There is no God but God and Mohammed is His prophet." The Koran is a little smaller than our New Testament, contains 114 chapters and was originally written in musical Arabic. It relates many stories from the Old Testament and some from the

New Testament, opposes idolatry, teaches the resurrection and judgment of all peoples; it teaches that Christ was born of a virgin, credits His miracles and holds Him as a forerunner of Mohammed. It pictures heaven as a gigantic harem where the "black-eyed daughters of paradise are held out as a reward to the commonest inhabitants." This religion has spread with the sword and its devotees robbed, plundered and spoiled all countries within reach. They made religion an exterior matter and exalted sensualism. Moslems are fanatical, self-satisfied, proud, intolerant and lacking in any degree of humility. They believe in a degree of fatalism unheard of in the Western world and this has made it possible for them to fight their wars. They believe the Koran should be read only in the original Arabic and do not like to see it translated into any other language. What good there is in this religion is far outweighed by its bad.

THE BIBLE CONTRASTED WITH THESE BOOKS.

None of these books offers relief from suffering, while the Bible tells man of "a city which hath foundations whose builder and maker is God" and that it is possible to attain this reward; the Bible accounts are based on historical fact while the other books deal with imagined occurrences; the Bible teaches an inward change, the other sacred books teach only exterior religion; the Bible blesses little children, makes men strong, makes women pure and chaste, honors the aged and offers eternal life to all.

CONCLUSION.

The Bible is so far superior to these other books that there is no comparison. Its purity, consistency, lofty ethics, and profound philosophy; its quickening of conscience, presentation of a divine Savior and offer of comfort, hope and inspiration in every time of trouble eyen death itself—leads us to conclude that it is the Word of God and that all other "sacred books" are uninspired and whatever good they may have is borrowed from the religion which the Creator revealed to His servants.

INTERNAL EVIDENCES OF INSPIRATION

The Bible contains its own proof of its divine origin. It vindicates itself. Frequently well-meaning but poorly informed people have said, "We cannot prove the truthfulness of the Bible by the Book itself", and "It will do no good to read the Bible to an infidel, as he doesn't believe it anyway. He must be convinced with outside evidence". There is an abundance of external evidence but it is not needed to establish the divine origin of the Bible. No stronger arguments are needed than those which lie within the Book itself. An infidel will come as near being convinced by this internal evidence as by any external proof.

THE UNITY OF THE BIBLE

The Bible consists of sixty-six books written by about forty different men over a period of sixteen hundred years. It was written by kings, soldiers, shepherds, farmers and fishermen. It was begun by Moses in the lonely desert of Arabia and finished by John on the Isle of Patmos. Some of it was written in kings' palaces, some in shepherds' tents, some beside still waters and part of it was written in prison. Part of the Bible was written by highly educated men and part of it was written by unlettered fishermen. It was written in different languages and different countries. Yet, when all the books of the Bible are brought together they blend into one great whole. They are a unit, hence The Book. There are no contradictions; there is no discord. It is never necessary to rewrite the Bible and bring it up to date. It is always up to date and was free of errors from the beginning. These men could have written such a book only by divine guidance. Just as the materials for Solomon's temple joined perfectly together because they were prepared under the direction of a great architect, so the books of the Bible blend harmoniously because they were written under the direction of the Holy Spirit of God.

When one of the world's outstanding encyclopedias was published, the publishers had to bring out an additional volume the following year to correct the errors which got into the first edition. The great scholars of the world had worked faithfully but mistakes were found just as they are found in all human productions. Skeptics have been unable to find even one error in the Bible. There are no mistakes and contradictions. It must, therefore, be that God directed its writing.

> "Many years ago I entered the wonderful temple of God's revelation. I entered the portico of Genesis and walked down through the Old Testament Art Gallery where the pictures of Adam, Noah, Abraham, Isaac, Jacob, Moses and Joshua; Samuel and David and Daniel hung on the wall. I entered the music room of the Psalms where the Spirit swept the keyboard of nature and brought forth the dirge-like wail of the weeping prophet, Jeremiah; to the grand impassioned strains of Isaiah until it seemed that every reed and harp in God's organ of nature responded to the tuneful touch of David, the sweet singer of Israel. I entered the chapel of Ecclesiastes where the voice of the preacher was heard and passed into the conservatory of Sharon where the

lily of the valley's sweet scented spices filled and perfumed my life. I entered the business room of the proverbs and passed into the observatory room of the prophets where I saw many telescopes of various sizes, some pointing to far-off events but all concentrated upon the Bright and Morning star which was soon to rise over the moonlit hills of Judea for our salvation. I entered the audience room of the King of Kings and caught a vision from the standpoint of Matthew, Mark, Luke and John; I entered the Acts of Apostles where the Holy Spirit was doing His office work in the forming of the church; I passed into the correspondence room where sat Paul, Peter, James, Jude and John penning their epistles. I stepped into the Throne Room of Revelation where all towered into glittering Peaks. I got a vision of the King seated upon His throne in all His glory, and I cried:

'All hail the power of Jesus' name,
Let angels prostrate fall,
Bring forth the royal diadem
And crown Him Lord of All.'"

THE STYLE OF THE WRITINGS.

The Record of Doubt.

If the books of the Bible had been forgeries they would not have recorded the fears and doubts of their heroes. We are told how Peter denied the Lord thrice, how, when in prison, John's faith was so weak that he sent to inquire if Jesus were really the Christ. We read that the brothers

of Christ did not believe in Him at first and tried to pre-
vent Him from preaching; we read that Jesus was twice
rejected by the people of His home town. We read that
the apostles fell asleep in Gethsemane and that they ran
away when Christ was arrested. A false account would
not have included these things. Every admission of doubt
is an assurance of a correct account.

The Record of Wrong-doing.

False books exalt their heroes. Their follies and sins are
not mentioned. But in the Bible the truth is told. Abraham is called the father of the faithful; yet, when he lied,
God had that recorded. When Moses, after leading Israel
for forty years, sinned and was prevented from entering
Canaan, God said, "Tell it all". Aaron, the high priest
made a golden calf for the people to worship; King Saul
was cruel and sinful; Elijah ran from Jezebel and the
apostles possessed human weaknesses. H. L. Hastings in
telling how God reported the evil deeds of His servants
says, "When the Lord undertakes to tell His story of a
sinful man, He does not select a poor, miserable beggar,
and show him up; He does not even give the name of the
thief on the cross, nor the wretched outcast who bathed
the Savior's feet with her tears; but He takes King David
from the throne, and sets him down in sackcloth and ashes and wrings from his heart the cry, "Have mercy upon
me, O God, according to Thy loving-kindness; according
to the multitude of Thy mercies blot out my transgres-
sions.' And when he is pardoned, forgiven, cleansed, and
made whiter than the snow, the pen of inspiration writes
down the whole dark, damning record of his crimes; and
the king on his throne has not the power, nor wealth, nor

influence enough to blot out the page; and it goes into history for the infidels to scoff at for three thousand years. Who wrote that?"

Familiar details.

The Bible abounds in familiar details which a literary forger would never think to invent. The woman wiping Jesus' feet with her hair; John outrunning Peter to the tomb but waiting outside while the impetuous Peter rushed in; Rhoda running to tell of Peter's knock without first letting him in; Paul sending for his books and coat; the linen cloth that had been around the Savior's head lying apart from the shroud. These simple, personal details simply mean that we are reading an honest and truthful account of what really happened. The books of the Bible bear no earmarks of forged documents.

THE PICTURE OF CHRIST.

How could a set of forgers paint such a picture of a God-man that the world has since worshipped Him? Did Shakespeare invent such a character? Did the combined wisdom of Goethe, Dante and Milton do it? How impossible that a set of forgers could picture a man with such wisdom, majesty and love that all the world would bow at His feet! No one could picture Christ as do the Bible writers save those who were close to Him in the flesh.

> "Here is a man who was born in an obscure village, the child of a peasant woman. He grew up in an obscure village. He worked in a carpenter shop until He was thirty, and then for three years He

was an itinerant teacher. He never wrote a book. He never held an office. He never owned a home. He never had a family. He never went to college. He never traveled two hundred miles from the place where he was born. He never did one of the things that usually accompany greatness.

"He had no credentials but Himself. He had nothing to do with this world except the power of His divine manhood. While still a young man, the tide of popular opinion turned against Him. His friends ran away. One of them denied Him. He was turned over to His enemies. He went through the mockery of a trial. He was nailed upon a cross between two thieves. His executioners gambled for the only piece of property He had on earth while He was dying His coat. Then He was taken down and laid in a borrowed grave through the love of a friend.

"Nineteen wide centuries have come and gone. Today He is the centerpiece of the human race and the leader of the column of progress. I am far within the mark when I say that all the armies that ever marched, and all the parliaments that ever sat, and all the kings that ever reigned, put together, have not affected the life of man upon this earth as powerfully as has that one solitary life." (Phillips Brooks).

What the Book Means to Human Hearts.

"This book contains...the mind of God, the state of man, the way of salvation, the doom of sinners. Its doctrines are holy, its precepts are binding, it histo-ries are true and its decisions immutable. Read it to be wise, believe it to be safe, and practice it to be holy. It contains light to direct you, food to support you and comfort to cheer you. It is the traveller's map, the pilgrim's staff, the pilot's compass, the soldier's sword, the Christian's charter. Here para-dise is restored, Heaven opened and the gates of Hell disclosed. Christ is its grand object, our good its design and the glory of God its end. It should fill the memory, rule the heart and guide the feet. Read it slowly, frequently and prayerfully. It is a mine of wealth, a paradise of glory and a river of pleasure. It is given you in life, will be open at the judgment and will be remembered forever. It in-volves the highest responsibility, rewards the greatest labor, and condemns all who trifle with its holy contents." (Anonymous).

The Bible
"Blessed Bible, how I love it!
How it doth my bosom cheer!
What hath earth like this to covet?
Oh, what stores of wealth are here!

"Man was lost and doomed to sorrow,
Not one ray of light or bliss
Could he from earth's treasures borrow
Till his way was cheered by this.

"Yes, I'll to my bosom press thee,
Precious Word, I'll hide thee here,

Sure my heart will ever bless thee,
For thou sayest 'Good cheer'.

"Speak my heart and tell thy ponderings,
Tell how far thy rovings led,
When this Book brought back thy wonderings,
Speaking life as from the dead.

"Yes, sweet Bible, I will hide thee,
Hide thee richly in this heart;
Thou through all my life will guide me,
And in death we will not part!

"Part in death! No, never, never!
Through death's vale I'll lean on thee;
Then in worlds above forever
Sweeter still thy truths shall be."
-Anonymous

THE INDESTRUCTABILITY OF THE BIBLE

DOWN through the centuries enemy after enemy has come forth to war against the Book of God. It has been gloriously triumphant over everyone, therefore, we believe it to be God's Word.

JUDAISM.

Throughout the Old Testament period the Book of the Lord suffered in the hands of its friends. Many times the Old Testament was openly attacked and often it was neglected. King Jehoiakim had part of Jeremiah's prophecy cut in pieces and cast into the fire. (Jeremiah 36). Antiochus IV, in 100 B.C., gathered all the Testaments he could find and burned them. He put to death all who retained a copy. (1 Macc. 1:27-28).

After the New Testament was written, Judaism fought a fierce battle with Christianity. The early disciples were Jews and it was difficult to get them to realize that the gospel must go to all nations. Paul rebuked the Christians for going back under the yoke of bondage; he withstood Peter and Barnabas. The church always had a tendency to Judaize.

Judaism was not only a force inside the church but a formidable enemy outside. Stephen and James, the brother of the Lord, were killed; Peter was imprisoned. Slaughter and threatening were breathed out against the disciples of the Lord and they were bound and cast into prison. Saul of Tarsus helped in the persecution but after his conversion he himself was stoned, starved, hated, persecuted, hunted, betrayed, imprisoned and beaten with thirty-nine stripes on five different occasions.

Forty years after the crucifixion of the Messiah, Judaism itself was destroyed. The saber has long been rusty in its heart, its adherents are scattered throughout the world and are themselves the victims of cruel persecutions.

HEATHENISM.

PRIESTS.

Heathenism was once a powerful force in the world. Hallowed by tradition and ennobled by patriotism; beautified by architecture and literature, it gripped the fancy of the nations. Heathenism became a religion for the people wherever it spread. "It adjusted itself to the beautiful in Greece, to the mysterious in Egypt, to the warlike in Rome, to the luxury of the East and did it as easily and naturally as the limpid waters of the sea adjust themselves to cliff and crag and sandy beach."

Rome became the center of heathenism. Hundreds of temples and chapels were in the city. Nearly every prominent man in Rome was a heathen priest or officeholder. To attack heathenism at Rome meant to strike at the tap root of it. Paul, the mighty soldier of the cross, went to Rome. He went not riding in a chariot with flaming steeds and captives chained to the wheels but as an old man suffering with disease and stricken with poverty. He was a prisoner chained to a rough, Roman soldier. But he conquered! Heathenism, the imperial mistress of the world, fell! From the time Paul entered Rome, the heathen temples began to close and today the glory of heathenism has departed. Heathen priests no longer control the world and grip the fancy of the nations.

PHILOSOPHERS.

The Roman sword captured Greece but the Grecian philosophers captured the minds of borne. Plato, Aristotle, Zeno and Epicurus divided among themselves the intellectual realms of Rome. "Whoever pretended to learning or virtue was their disciple; the greatest magistrates, generals, kings ranged themselves under their disciples, were trained up in their schools and professed the opinions they taught." (Lyttelton). "From the Portico the Roman civilians learned to live, to reason and to die." (Gibbon).

The philosophical culture of the world arrayed itself against the Bible and attempted by argument and ridicule to refute it. Pliny, the Governor; Marcus Aurelius, the Emperor; Tacitus, the historian and dozens of others wrote argument, ridicule, sneer and merciless attack against the Bible. They tried to tell men that life is futile, that the problem of whence came man and whither he goes cannot be solved. But man had enough woes of his own without borrowing from these heathen philosophers. Their works were ably refuted by Christians living at the time and today their glory has departed. The Bible is absolute master of the field. It tells man of trouble, sin, sickness and sorrow but it reminds him that he has a glorious origin and that when all the battles have been fought and all the victories won he will not slumber in the cold embrace of death but that he has a glorious destiny. Every system of ancient philosophy is dead; the Bible lives!

> "It is true that a little philosophy inclines a man's mind to Atheism; But depth in Philosophy brings men's minds about to Religion: For while the mind of man looks upon Second Causes scattered, it may sometimes rest in them and goes no farther: But when it beholds the chain of them confederate and linked together, it must needs fly to Providence and Deity." (Bacon, Essay XVI).

EMPERORS.

The kings and emperors of the world brought their combined influence and power to bear upon the Bible that they might destroy it and banish Christianity from the earth. Heathen priest and philosopher had failed to kill Christianity but, ah, wait for the power of persecution.

Claudius, A.D. 41-54, banished many Christians from Rome; Nero, in A.D. 64, sewed Christians in the skins of wild animals and had them torn to pieces by dogs, he crucified many, some he tied to high posts, their bodies covered with pitch, and set fire to them to light the streets while his friends drove merrily by; Domitian, 81-96, killed many Christians and even exiled his wife for becoming one.

Under Trajan, 98-117, Bishop Simeon was crucified at Jerusalem and Ignatius of Antioch was killed. Under Marcus Aurelius, Polycarp was burned to death for not denying the Lord whom he had served for eighty-six years. At Lyons, France, Bishop Pothinus, more than ninety years old, died in a loathsome prison from the effects of abuse. Many others were tortured and killed there.

Septimius Severus, 193-211, had Leonidas, father of Origen, beheaded at Alexandria. Ptaminea and her mother, Marcella, were slowly dipped in seething oil.

The story is the same under Decius and Gallus, 251-253, and Valerianus, 253-260. The latter made a specialty of killing preachers. At Carthage, Cyprian and Laurentius were commanded to bring forth the treasures of the church. They brought the poor, the infirm, and the orphans and were roasted alive for this affront to their ruler.

Diocletian, 284-305, had a Christian wife and daughter, yet he persecuted Christians. All churches were destroyed, meetings forbidden and the Emperor made a hobby of burning Bibles and killing their owners. Christians were accused of starting a fire in the Emperor's palace and all over the empire were tortured. Galerius continued this persecution in 305. Christianity grew! Finally, the emperor issued an edict in 311 tolerating Christianity and asking the Christians to pray for him.

Maximus renewed the persecution of Christians. He burned their buildings and killed their leaders. He published the Acta Pilati, a book slandering the sufferings of Christ and introduced it as a textbook in the schools that the minds of the young might be poisoned

When Licinius courted the favor of the pagans, his rival, Constantine, declared himself a Christian and took down the eagle to put up the cross. He declared himself in favor of Christianity because it had already conquered his people.

It seems that with all this persecution, Christianity would have perished but it did not. God watched over it. Fifty days after the crucifixion of Christ, twelve unlettered men stood in the city of Jerusalem and with power from on high unfurled the blood-stained banner of Christ. Three thousand souls were added to the church that day. The number of the disciples "grew and multiplied". When the disciples were scattered abroad "they went everywhere preaching the word". Within five years there were churches throughout Palestine. Within eight years both Jews and Gentiles were Christians. Within forty years the gospel had been preached in every known nation. The world had been turned upside down. Throughout Asia Minor, Greece, Italy, the Isles of the Aegean and the sea coast of Africa there were thousands of Christians. No wonder, then, that Constantine declared himself in favor of Christianity!

Julian the Apostate, Constantine's nephew, renounced Christianity in 351 when he was twenty years old and ten years later openly championed heathenism. He ruled for a year and a half and wrote a Refutation of the Christian Religion in which he collected the arguments of the infidels who had lived before him. In attacking the New Testament he bears valuable testimony for it. In a war with the Persians, he died June 25, 363. His dying words were, "O Galilean, Thou hast conquered!"

HERESY.

The Bible has been betrayed in every generation by those who were supposed to be its friends. The Manichees, the Gnostics, the Donatists and others attacked the Bible. Arius, an elder at Alexandria, declared that Christ was not the true God. He led many Christians away from the truth. There have ever been apostate leaders and apostate sects but the church has lived and the truth has prevailed.

BARBARISM.

Attila, the Hun; Genseric, the Vandal; Alaric, the Goth and the hordes with them surged over civilization and it seemed that the Bible would perish. Gibbon says, "The progress of Christianity has been marked by two glorious and decisive victories, over the learned and luxurious civilization of the Roman Empire and over the warlike barbarians of Scythia and Germany, who subverted the empire and embraced the religion of the Romans." (Vol. 3, p. 158).

MOHAMMEDANISM.

As a religion Mohammedanism is a gigantic plagiarism. It is a combination of heathenism, Judaism and Christianity with but little of the latter. It is Judaism adapted to Arabia, recognizing Jesus and Mahomet as prophets. The Koran is in no way comparable to the Bible but as a military theocracy the Crescent has always warred against the Cross. In 732 the Crescent was carried in battle to within a few miles of Paris and was beaten back by Charles

Martel in the battle of Tours. Again and again the soldiers of Mohammedanism have tried to destroy all Bibles and kill all Christians. Today Mohammedanism is a force to be reckoned with but when the last chapter of history has been written, who can doubt but that Christianity will prevail?

THE PAPACY.

At no time has the Bible been in greater danger than when the Popes of Rome held world-wide power Instead of spreading the Bible they suppressed it.

Pope Innocent III, in 1199, had the French Bibles burned at Metz and forbade the people to have more. The Council of Tarragona, in Spain, under Pope Gregory IX in 1234, ordered the people to bring in their Bibles so they might be burned. Ferdinand and Isabella, 1474-1516, forbade the people to have Bibles. Wyclif was condemned for heresy by the Synod of Oxford in 1383 because he translated the Bible. Clarks IV issued an edict against German Bibles in 1369. Pope Julius III was advised in 1553 by a number of bishops to permit the least possible reading of the Bible in order that the Papacy might be strengthened. Cardinal Paul Vergerius later reported this when he became a Protestant.

Ten thousand Bibles were burned at Graez in Steiermark on August 8, 1600 by order of Ferdinand II, who had been emperor. The Jesuits boasted of burning 60,000 Bibles in a single year—1637—in Bohemia. Pope Clement II, in 1713, condemned Bible reading on the part of Christians. Pope Pius VI did likewise. Pope Pius VII called the Bible societies a pest in 1816. Pope Gregory XVI, on May 6, 1844, said those favoring Bible societies were guilty of the greatest crime before God and the church.

The Popes repeatedly condemned all reading of scriptures except in the Latin language and discouraged that. In the fifteenth century, priests became atheists and scoffed at the doctrines of the Bible; scholars filled their writings with blasphemy; immorality was abundant; Leo X jested with his secretary about the profitableness of the fable of Christ. Many church leaders denied the immortality of the soul.

But from the midst of darkness and degradation the power of God rescued the Bible and the Beacon Light shines on. In 1939 the Bible was translated into its thousandth language and already one of the Bible societies is putting it into fifteen more. Five hundred years ago the body of Wycliffe was dug up, burned and his ashes thrown into the brook Swift all because he had once translated the Bible. Tonstal, Bishop of London, had thousands of copies of Tyndale's English New Testament bought and burned at the cross of St. Paul's Cathedral. Tyndale used the money to print more and the Bishop decided that burning the Bible was only advertising it. Bishop Nikke wrote, "It passeth my power or that of any spiritual man to hinder it now, and if this continues much longer, it will undo us all." Yea, verily!

MODERN INFIDELITY.

Modern infidelity is simply the same old foe—unbelief—which has always warred against Christianity. Is it not interesting that Christianity and the Bible have been "destroyed" countless times and yet the process must be repeated every generation?

In the seventeenth and eighteenth centuries the Bible light was all but extinguished and the nations of Europe walked by what they called "reason". And are these pages from history a sample of the much boasted "improvement" which infidels want to give the world? In Prussia, Frederick II made his royal court a cesspool of infidelity and broadcasted it over the land. In England, Blackbourne, Archbishop of York, told Queen Caroline he had been talking to Walpole about the new mistress "and was glad to find Her Majesty was such a sensible woman as to like her husband should divert himself." Cave says, "I beheld religion laid waste and Christianity ready to draw its last breath, stifled and oppressed with the vice and impiety of a debauched and profligate age." In Russia, Catherine II was indeed "That foul woman of the North. The lustful murderess of her wedded Lord."

In France the kings let adulteresses influence the nation more than the profoundest scholars and wisest statesmen. The reign of terror came with Robespierre and Paine. The Christian religion was abolished by law and a harlot was proclaimed the Goddess of Reason. In 1793 the French passed a law legislating God out of existence but in 1794 they found it necessary to recall Him. Robespierre cried, "If God did not exist, 'twere well to invent Him."

Modern infidels have tried hard to bury the Bible but it will not stay buried. Voltaire, the French skeptic, (1694-1778), said, "In less than a hundred years the Bible will be discarded and Christianity swept from the earth." Time has proved him to be a false prophet. His writings have a modest circulation. His old printing press has been used to print Bibles and his house has been used as a depot by an international Bible society.

Thomas Paine, a Quaker preacher and a firm believer in God and the Bible while in America as shown by his own writings, went to France in 1787 and became an infidel. He wrote a book, The Age of Reason, which he said would destroy the Bible and Christianity. If it had any effect on either it was never noticed. Paine died in 1809 and the Bible which he fought goes marching triumphantly on.

In America in 1885 Colonel Robert G. Ingersoll prophesied that in a quarter of a century no more churches would be built. He traveled over the country and lectured on "The Mistakes of Moses" but it would be far more interesting to hear Moses speak on "The Mistakes of Colonel Ingersoll". His career in the army would shame a coward. His morals may be compared to those of the French infidels whom he imitated. His speeches were taken from their books. Ingersoll was challenged to debate all over the country by dozens of reputable Christians and Jews but always refused.

IT LIVES!

Christians believe the Bible is God's Word because it cannot be destroyed. Evil men have hated it from the beginning. Every doctrine in it has been hated and every verse has been attacked. Any human product would have perished long ago under such a withering attack, but the Bible lives and has a greater hold on humanity than ever before. Forty million copies are printed annually—forty thousand times as many copies of the Bible are circulated as any other book. When the Revised Version appeared on May 1, 1881, over a million copies were sold that day.

Every few years somebody demolishes the Bible, proves it "false" and completely "explodes it". Yet, the pieces come together and are stronger than ever. The Bible is like the Irishman's fence. He had put up the fence many times only to see it torn down. Finally, he built a fence of cement and stone, three feet high and four feet wide. When asked the reason for this strange fence, he said, "I built it three feet high, and four feet wide so it will be higher when it is turned over." Let the skeptics attack the blessed old Book. It will be higher when they finish! Aye, let them criticize. Christians are indebted to the attacks of skeptics for these attacks have called forth an ever-increasing number of arguments in favor of the Bible. Yes, indeed, "the more the truth is rubbed the brighter it will shine".

The Bible is like the anvil which wears out many hammers and remains unblemished.

"Last eve I passed beside a blacksmith's door
And heard the anvil ring the vesper chime;
When looking in, I saw upon the floor,
Old hammers worn with beating years of time.

"'How many anvils have you had,' said I,
'To wear and batter all these hammers so?
'Just one,' said he; then said with twinkling eye,
'The anvil wears the hammers out, you know.'

"And so, I thought, the anvil of God's word
For ages skeptics' blows have beat upon;
Yet, though the noise of falling blows was heard,
The anvil is unharmed—the hammers gone!"

Into every country of the world believers are going with the Word of God. Its blessed influence is gaining strength and power and when the last battle has been fought and the last victory has been won; when the last attack has been made and the last drop of martyr's blood has been shed; when the last song has been sung and the last prayer has been prayed, the earth will melt with fervent heat and the skies shall be rolled up as a scroll but Christians will stand before the Lord, the Righteous Judge, and see opened their Book which guided their weary feet and brought them at last safely home. "Even so, come Lord Jesus." Amen!

www.ingramcontent.com/pod-product-compliance
Lightning Source LLC
Chambersburg PA
CBHW061730020426

42331CB00006B/1184